Log Cabin Grub Cookbooks

900 E Carnation Drive
Sandy, UT 84094-4533
Phone: 801-571-0789 Office
       801-557-0798 Cell

THANKS FOR BUYING OUR LOG CABIN COOKBOOKS.
Currently (or soon to be) available.

1. Log Cabin Grub
2. Dutch Oven Black Pot Cookin
3. Log Cabin Campfire
4. Holidays & Traditions
5. Lewis & Clark
6. One Potato Two Potato
7. Dutch Oven Fish Book (*soon*)

SECTIONS	
1-16	Information
17-48	Main Meals
49-80	Breads
81-112	Desserts & Veggies
113-128	Misc.

Helpful hints are found throughout this book. Don't miss our Buffalo Company Soup on page 23, Preserving Walnuts on page 120, all about soap on page 124, Start your own Sour Dough on pages 59 and 60, Cattails - the hidden vegetable on pages 72 and 73, Finger type measurements on page 57, Make you own Bisquick also on page 57, and much, much more.

August 2010
9th Printing

Author: Colleen Sloan

Introduction

I don't really think this book needs an introduction, but I would like to tell you what a challenge it has been to complete it. I have reached a goal that I set for myself about 30 years ago when I talked my Grandmother out of her Oatmeal Cookie recipe. A very good friend named Karen H. gave me lots of help and inspirations. These recipes were gathered over many years and handed down from relatives. Cooking has always been fun for me, and my family has been my greatest taste testers. When grandma and my mom cooked it was a puzzle to try and figure out how much a fistful of flour and a pinch of salt really was. I am a Great Granddaughter of the Pioneers and very active in the Scouting program. These 2 hobbies help me to try new recipes all the time. Many a time I've tried to get my boys to try Cattail flapjacks and Dandelion salad. You really should try them to find out if you could live like they used too. The taste is quite pleasant and the experience is worthwhile. I hope that you will enjoy the book and all the helpful hints that I have put inside. I have tried every recipe and know that every gourmet recipe had to come from somewhere, and I believe they started with good basic cookin.

I dedicated this book to my son LARRY and to his love for camping & cooking. To the rest of my children, LISA, STEVE, DUSTIN & JUSTIN for the taste testing they have endured and to my friends for their support and belief in my ability to do it. Especially John.

To those of you who buy one of these cookbooks, you've just made a COUNTRY GIRL'S dream come true.

Thanks for buying our Book. Cook with Love "COLLEEN"

Good common judgment in all outdoor activities is the key to a successful camp.

Index

Introduction 2

"Let's Talk About Vinegar" ... 6

All About the Book 8

Cast-Iron History 9

Judging the Right Temperature 10

Cleaning Your Dutch Oven 12

Care and Storing of your Oven 13

Stacking Dutch Ovens 14

Seasoning Your Dutch Oven... 15

Accessorize Your Dutch Oven 16

Barbecue Sauce for all Meats 17

Old Fashion Deer Jerky 17

Log Cabin Chicken Pie 18

Prairie Chicken or Sage Grouse 19

You Wish Chicken Legs 19

Mulligan Stew 20

Stewed Chicken 20

Wild Game Birds 21

Sage Dressing by Granny 21

Wild Game Jerky 22

Venison 22

Roast Leg 22

Buffalo Company Soup 23

Jackrabbit Stew...................... 23

Cowboy Stew 24

Never Fail Dumplings 24

Squeak Bubble and Meat........ 25

Making Corn Beef................... 25

Country Pot Roast 26

Sheepherder Leftover Pie 26

Mrs. Hales Requested Meat Loaf 27

Short-ribs and Dumplings....... 27

Mincemeat for Every Use....... 28

Dutch Oven Baked Beans....... 28

Chili from Way Back 29

Chili Wheat 30

Sweet Crackers (1720) 30

Pork & Sweet Potato Pie........ 31

Onion Biscuits 31

Porky's Pie Crust 32

Meat Pie Possibles.................. 32

Catalina Island Chicken......... 33

Skillet Pork Chops.................. 33

"Buffalo" 34

Apple Dressing for Birds 35

Baked Woodchuck 35

Southern Chestnut Dressing .. 35

Wagon Wheel Beans 36

Fried Rabbit............................ 36

Dumplings 37

Mountaineer Stew................... 37

Fried Woodchuck.................... 38

Ground Hog or Beaver........... 38

Opossum or Raccoon 38

Squirrel Soup 38

Rattlesnake Stew 39

Fish Dressing 40

Fish Cakes............................... 41

Frog Legs – Jumpin Gimminy ... 42

Potato Cakes with Vegetables 42

Dutch Oven Baked Beans....... 43

Stuffed Turnips....................... 43

Pope Bailey's Jambalaya......... 44

Baking a Chicken.................... 46

Log Cabin Chicken Soup 46

Turkey Noodle Casserole 47

Chicken or Turkey Hash 47

Pork Chili Verde 48

Quick and Easy Chili and Cornbread 48

Squaw Bread 49

Western Poor Man's Bread.... 50

Hobo Bread in Loafs 50

Injun Fry Bread...................... 51

Basic Dutch Oven Bread 51

Curly-Q-Pretzels 52

Index

FARMERS BREAD.........................52

OLD FASHION POTATO BREAD.....53

YAM BISCUITS 53

COUNTRY QUICK ROLLS OR BREAD 54

OATMEAL TRAIL MUFFINS 54

BUTTERMILK IRISH SODA BREAD .55

PUMPKIN DAY BREAD 55

SODA CRACKERS.........................56

RANCHHAND SUPREME ROLLS......56

LOG CABIN BAKING MIX 57

CAMP BISCUITS...........................57

BASIC EGG NOODLES 57

CHUCKWAGON BISCUITS 58

THE REAL MEADOW MUFFINS 58

SOURDOUGH STARTER WITHOUT YEAST 59

STARTER WITH YEAST 59

SOURDOUGH SCRATCH START 60

SERGEANT BOBS PANCAKES.........60

MOUNTAIN MUFFINS 61

WINTER SNOW HOTCAKES 61

CRACKERS FOR SNACKS...............61

COW COUNTRY BUTTERMILK PANCAKES 62

MAPLE SYRUP 62

SPOON BREAD 63

ROUND-UP MUFFINS...................63

BREAK-APART CORNBREAD..........64

GRANNY CARLSONS JOHNNY CAKES 64

SOUTHWEST CORN BREAD 65

CORNBUCK BREAD......................65

PILGRIM'S BREAD 66

INDIAN ZUNI BREAD 66

FALL AND WINTER SQUASH BREAD 67

ROCKY EDGE POPOVERS..............67

FRESH APPLE BREAD...................68

NUT GRAHAM BREAD 68

DANISH EBLESKEWERS 69

SIMPLE FRITTERS 69

DANISH STOLLEN BREAD.............70

ON THE TRAIL DONUTS 71

CARROT BREAD 71

CATTAILS – OUR FREE FOOD - AVAILABLE 72

CATTAIL FLAPJACKS....................73

HAPPINESS CAKE 74

LEFTOVER HAM CANAPES............74

SALT RISING POTATO WATER BREAD 76

LEFTOVER BREAD DRESSING FOR CHICKEN 76

POTATO RANCH ROLLS................77

QUICK POTATO BREAD................77

LEFTOVER CORNMEAL ZUCCHINI MUFFINS 78

SOUR MILK BISCUITS 78

SOUR MILK BRAN MUFFINS 79

LEFTOVER SOUR CREAM BISCUITS 79

HUSH PUPPIES 80

PONEHAWS 80

PAPA NILES CHOCOLATE SAUERKRAUT CAKE 81

HOMEMADE MAYO CAKE 81

DO WITHOUT CAKE 82

HICKORY NUT SPICE CAKE..........82

AUTUMN SQUASH CAKE 83

APPLE PIE HARVEST CAKE 83

CREEK WATER CAKE 84

WASHINGTON'S CURRANT DELIGHT 84

OLD FARM FRUIT CAKE 85

ON THE TRAIL APPLESAUCE CAKE 85

GRANDMA'S BOILED FRUITCAKE ..86

FRUIT CAKE SPICED COOKIES 86

MAMA'S JELLYROLL DELIGHT......87

BLACKBERRY SHORTCAKE 87

OATMEAL CAKE TOPPING 88

JELLY MEETING DAY CAKE.........88

BROWN BETTY – GRANNY'S WAY 88

HUCKLEBERRY OR ELDERBERRY PIE 89

Index

RHUBARB COUNTRY PIE 89

CURRANT OR GOOSEBERRY DOUBLE CRUST PIE 90

GRANNY'S GOOSEBERRY PIE 90

GRANDMA'S PUMPKIN PIE SURPRIZE 91

SOUTHERN RAISIN PIE 91

SUGAR YUM YUM PIE 92

MERINGUE 92

UNCLE CY'S VINEGAR PIE 92

KOHLRABI WITH CREAM SAUCE ... 93

BARROOM CARROTS 93

CARROTS – THE MIRACLE VEGETABLE 94

GLAZED CARROTS 94

COOKED CARROTS 94

KAREN'S CARROT PIE 95

HOT WATER PIE CRUST 95

SHOO FLY PIE 95

GREEN TOMATO PIE 96

WHATEVER FRUIT PIE 96

AUNT LOU'S MINCEMEAT COOKIES 97

COWBOY COOKIES 97

CARROT COOKIES OLD FASHIONED 98

LEFTOVER BREADCRUMB COOKIES 98

LOUISA'S OATMEAL DROP COOKIES 99

LOUISA'S OATMEAL CAKE 99

SQUASH COOKIES 100

HERDER BRAN COOKIES 100

GINGERSNAPS 100

GRANNY'S CINNAMON CRISPS 100

FRESH MOUNTAIN BLUEBERRY COBBLER 101

COBBLER CRUST 101

LEFT OVER CORN PUDDING #2 102

BLUEBERRY PUDDING CAKE 102

APPLE FRITTERS 103

APPLE DUMPLINGS 103

OLD HOME PUDDING MIX 104

COUNTRY BREAD PUDDIN 104

PRAIRIE PUDDING 105

RHUBARB PUDDING 105

OLD SQUAW INDIAN PUDDING 106

BAKED RHUBARB 107

STUFFED ONIONS 107

WATERCRESS SOUP 108

QUICK COUNTRY CARROTS 108

CACTUS JELLY 109

CACTUS CANDY 110

MARSHMALLOWS 111

MALLOW CORN AND NUTS 111

WATER CRESS -- ROOMY SALAD .. 111

CORN MEAL MUSH - FRIED 112

HOARHOUND CANDY 112

HOT BUTTERED RUM 114

SWEETENED CONDENSED MILK 114

NUT BRITTLE 115

WHITE TAFFY 115

CRACKER JACKS 116

EASY TO MAKE POPCORN BALLS . 116

WHITE SAUCE 117

INSTANT WHITE SAUCE 117

GRAHAM CRACKERS 118

LOG CABIN NOODLES 118

HOMEMADE MAYONNAISE 119

BAKED PEACHES 120

SNOW ICE CREAM 120

BRINE FOR CURING MEAT 121

POTATO CHIPS 121

POULTRY SEASONING 121

DANDELION COFFEE 122

GREENS 122

BUTTERMILK TIPS FOR COOKING .. 123

OLD WESTERN GREEN TOMATO CATSUP 125

DANDELION GREEN SALAD 125

FRIED TOMATOES 125

TOMATO SOUP 126

9-MILE HERITAGE EXPEDITIONS ... 127

OTO RANCH INFORMATION 128

"Let's Talk About Vinegar"

Vinegar is one of the items I always take with me when I leave home. "**NATURAL APPLE CIDER VINEGAR**", that is. <u>I mix the vinegar in a spray bottle at a 4 to 1 mixture</u> (4 parts water to 1 part vinegar). It serves as a tenderizer and a disinfectant. And, as you know, anything tender cooks faster. Spraying the vinegar solution on meats and vegetables will kill all the bacteria that forms at room temperature. Spraying it on your pots, will disinfect them and make them easier to clean. Spraying it on your hands and on the cooking surface you use is also a safe way to go.

Taking a spray bottle of vinegar-water with you when you go camping, is a good idea also. It's a disinfectant for cuts, scrapes and bites. You can treat sunburns by spraying them lightly every few minutes to cool the burn and let the heat out. I don't know about your camp trips, but my 5 kids had their share of accidents. When my son Steve fell 20 feet through the Quakie branches and ran a branch thru his hand, the vinegar water helped to keep the infection out and allowed it to heal.

One time Justin, one of my twins, got a fish hook in his finger and we had to freeze it to get it out. Another time one was imbedded so far in we had to take Dustin into Pinedale to have it removed. A dentist was the only one available, and right after he finished a root canal on his dog, he helped Dustin. By soaking the hand and keeping the wound disinfected and the skin tender, it allowed the hand to heal with no scar. Soaking sore tired feet in warm vinegar water mixed 3 to 1 helps to relax the muscles and relieve the ache. Soaking feet helps to remove calluses and soften skin so that blisters won't form. Soaking hands in warm vinegar water, softens skin and removes hang nails. It also keeps infections out of rose bush scratches and cactus stings. Vinegar

"Look for No Trace Camping Tips throughout this book."

Page: 6

is available in most stores. I take a tbsp. of vinegar in a little water every morning to help tenderize my joints and give me energy. It helps to relieve the arthritis pain in my hands. Vinegar kills bacteria in water, so - it's a good thing to take camping. Use it in your rinse water for dishes. Make VINEGAR a household word in your home, "The pioneers did."

Apple cider vinegar is a marvelous combination of tart good taste and germ killing acids. It is fermented from sweet apple cider and takes its color from the tannins which flow from the ruptured cell walls of ripe apples. Apple Cider Vinegar contains more than thirty important nutrients, a dozen minerals, over a dozen vitamins and essential acids and several enzymes. Plus, it has a large dose of pectin for a healthy heart. Apple vinegar with sweet energy laden honey, is a supportive measure that encourages the body to defend itself from sickness. This combination can be used to help lower cholesterol. And, vinegar is said to shift the body's gears into low. Protecting us from stress related illness. A stronger dose of vinegar and honey (2 tbsp. vinegar + 2 tbsp. honey) in a glass of water and taken every morning is proven to lower cholesterol and normalize blood pressure. Through the ages, vinegar and honey has been prescribed as an aid in maintaining good general health, controlling diseases such as arthritis, and controlling weight. Both honey and vinegar contain large amounts of potassium. Neither are considered a drug, but are pure natural foods that promote the body's ability to help itself. Drinking a glass of water with 2 tsp. of vinegar and honey curb's the appetite before a meal and promotes good health. New research is beginning to show the wonderful effects or Vinegar and Honey. For good health and general well being, try vinegar and honey.

Simmer 1/2 cup vinegar in a pot of water to sweeten the air and absorb the oders indoors.

All About the Book

About the Book Layout:

This book was designed with the average camper in mind.

The recipes have been placed head to head in order for the book to be read in a standing position. This makes the book more readable when you are changing pages. A campfire cookbook is usually hung from the cook box or over a tree branch. There is hardly ever a place to lay it flat.

Try this; most of us take bungee cords camping, so get some real small ones like in this picture, and you can hang the cookbook from any nail or branch.

Wilderness Awareness

Since I have been involved with the NO-TRACE Camp Schools in Missoula Mt. at the **Nine Mile Historic Ranger Station**, I cannot believe how my awareness of the wilderness has improved. I am conscious more than ever of how people treat the out of doors. I try to encourage my Dutch Oven classes to get involved and show others how to care for our natural resources. The Rangers and teachers of the personnel that represent the KNOL'Ss program are very special people and know their stuff.

The Scouting programs stress the importance of this way of life in the back country, but a little help from all my friends that read this book would help to make our outdoor experiences worth having. Do your part to help keep our country clean, and if you're ever near Missoula, Mt. be sure to drop in and see the **Historic 9-Mile Ranger Station** and take the tour. Tell them Colleen sent you and they'll probably say, "WHO" [Just kidding].

Cast-Iron History

Early reference to the Black pots can be found in the old testament as Cauldron cooking. It is referred to as early as 4000 BC. Reports of Columbus coming to America also brought Black Pots to our attention. An early Oxford Dictionary, said that "pot", is the name given to a vessel that grows narrower towards the top, and "kettle" to the vessel that grows wider up top. A pot will except a lid easier that a Kettle. Shakespeare in about 1606, referred to boiling kettles and cauldrons in the witches scene of Macbeth. In 1620, when the pilgrims landed in Plymouth aboard the Mayflower, they were reported as cooking with the pots as they traveled. They built fires in sand pits and suspended the pots from the ships beams. This was easier than the stationary base supported pots, because the contents would slosh around with the sea movements. On real windy days, cooking would be suspended.

Until the start of the 18th century, iron was cast in baked loam or clay soil. This made for a rough surface and the mold generally broke after one casting. For many years, foundries were more advanced in the Holland area, and cast iron pots were imported to Britain. These early pots were very thick walled. In 1704, Abraham Darby traveled from Holland to inspect the foundries of England. From this trip the sand molds were perfected. In 1708, he received a patent for the process and soon after began to produce large quantities of cast iron pots in the furnace at Coalbrookdale. By the mid-eighteenth century, these pots were being shipped to the Americas. This joint venture with the Dutch pots resulted in the trading of pot salesmen throughout the colonies. When a trader was seen coming in his wagon, it was said, "Here comes the Dutchman with his ovens." Some were called Dinner pots, Gypsy pots, Bean pots, Stew pots and stock pots. By the late 1700's pots were being made in the American colonies also. Improvements came with a good lid and a flared edge to hold the coals on top. Some things have changed with the ovens but we still have an excellent cooking and browning pot that is very useful today. Cooking with the ovens and not lifting the lids will maintain 80% or more of the food value. These ovens are really a self timing pot. Learning to judge your heat and waiting for the smell will tell you when it's done.

Judging the Right Temperature

BAKING: When using the Black Pot to bake in, the heat must be distributed on the top and bottom to maintain the proper temperature. Usually a 300 to 350 degree temperature is sufficient to bake most any dish. If you are outside in the wind, it will take away some of your heat, but the following chart should help. You can raise or lower the temperature by adding 1 briquette for every 18 to 20 degrees you wish to add to the cooking temperature.

FRYING: For frying, boiling or steaming of any dish, there should be only bottom heat. If you wish to simmer for awhile, remove 1/2 of the heat from the bottom. A Tripod is an excellent tool for this type of cooking, because it is so easy to raise or lower against the heat. Using briquettes to cook with, will help to save the trees and open ground fires. With a DUTCH OVEN it is very easy to practice NO TRACE CAMPING. It is much easier to regulate your heat with briquettes than over an open fire. As your briquettes burn down, their heat also declines. To maintain the proper temperature, add briquettes as necessary to keep the heat fairly constant. A charcoal starter is excellent to keep briquettes always ready and available. My grandmother used to judge her stove temperature by throwing a two-finger pinch of flour in the oven. If the flour did not brown in 5 minutes, the stove temperature was less than 250 degrees. If it was brown in color, it meant that the oven was about 350 degrees and just right to bake bread. Most people have their own method of heat testing, but I have found the above chart to work well for me. I sincerely hope you will experiment with your oven and try many different dishes.

Your Dutch Oven will serve you well if you take proper care of it and treat it with respect.

Briquettes Only: When you are 2/3rds of the way through the baking recipe, remove the bottom heat except for 3 or 4 briquettes and this will prevent burning your food. The briquettes can be added to the top if necessary. If the top is browning to fast, remove 3 or 4 briquettes from the lid and allow baking to finish its time. Arranging the briquettes so that the heat remains even is also very important. Too much heat on one side will burn that spot and leave the middle not done. Baking can be a lot of fun in a Dutch Oven but proper heat and the 2/3rds rule are important factors.

Oven Size (in inches)	8"	10"	12"	14"	16"	22"
Top Heat	11	13	15	17	19	25

[Briquettes = Oven Size +3]

In your Volcano or collapsible stove, 12 Briquettes with no top heat will keep your oven at 350 to 375 degrees. Use the damper (Control ring) to control the burning rate of the briquettes.

Oven Size (in inches)	8"	10"	12"	14"	16"	22"
Bottom Heat	6	8	10	12	14	20

[Briquettes = Oven size - 2]

Gas Cooking: Cooking with propane or gas stoves can also be accomplished by using a flame tamer or heat defuser shield and a **Camp Chef Dutch Dome**. Then 85% of the heat is trapped under the dome and using low heat on the stove allows your pot to bake without burning. The heat plate fits over the burner and the pot is then placed on top. Even bread will bake up golder brown. Any **Camp Chef** stove will work like a charm.

Top   Bottom

Always place more heat on top than on the bottom when cooking with Briquettes only.

Cleaning Your Dutch Oven

On pages 6 and 7 we briefly touched on the care of your oven. A lot of people will tell you never to wash your pot with soap, but that is an old wives tale. When the pioneers used the pots, they did not have hot running water as we do today. Soap adheres to grease, but will release with hot water and rinse clean. I have a pot of my Dads that is over 75 years old and it has been washed several times. It has no legs and today still cooks as good as any of my brand new ones. These pots are not very fragile, but still require a certain amount of care. Dropping them or banging them against a hard surface could crack them and then their ability to hold the pressure and hot moisture diminishes.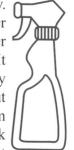

When you wash a pot, use only a mild detergent and always rinse thoroughly with hot water. It is important to heat your pan and thoroughly dry it before storing. I always clean my pans hot because it helps to release the food particles. I find it helpful to return the pot to the heat after emptying it, and spraying in a little Vinegar water to soften the food. Then I wipe it clean with paper towels and return it to the heat to dry. Always wipe out the excess grease with a clean paper towel. Store the pots in a dry place with a clean sheet of paper towel inside to keep the moisture from rusting your oven. You take care of them and they'll do you proud. The 1 part vinegar & 4 parts water is a great cleaning agent and disinfectant. The Apple Cider Vinegar is something I learned from my Pioneer Grandparents and mom.

You do not have to oil them to put them away if they are totally dry of moisture.

Remember that the only way to dry cast iron is to return the pot to the heat and evaporate the moisture.

Care and Storing of your Oven

When storing your oven, be sure that it has been thoroughly <u>dried with heat</u> on the stove after cleaning. Allow it to cool down & place a single paper towel inside to make sure that any moisture that forms will be absorbed. It is now ready to use again. When you need it next time, heat your oven and lightly grease it before you use it. If mine have gotten dusty or dirty, I will spray them with Vinegar water and wipe them out to disinfect them before I heat and grease them.

Oiling your ovens to put them away can cause the grease to go rancid. That is easily detected by the spoiled smell of the pot when opened. The grease actually goes rather yellow and looks like a gummy texture. Simply fill your oven with water & add a cup of apple cider Vinegar and boil for about 1/2-hour on the stove. Remove and dump out water. You should be able to scrape or scour out the rancid grease and then lightly oil while it is hot, and turn it upside down on a hot (400 or better) stove or your Volcano with 25 briquettes. If you have the storage bags they are nice to keep you ovens clean. I do not suggest plastic because it will make your oven sweat and cause rust. If your oven gets real rusty or you have a chance to pick one up at a garage sale that is real rusty, you can clean them with alfalfa, vinegar and water. Everyone has his or her secrets and you need to practice with your oven and do what suits you best. The more you try, the better it will get.

Like **Mama** used to say,

"Practice will make Perfection Happen".

Look up the "International Dutch Oven Society".
You'll be glad you did.

www.idos.com

Join us!

Stacking Dutch Ovens

Stacking the Dutch Ovens will depend on how many you intend to feed and if you are going to prepare more than a one dish meal. Stacking saves on briquettes, but the cooking times of each oven is also important. Your roast or spareribs may need 2 hours and bread only 45 minutes. Wind will have a tendency to make the briquettes burn hotter so be sure to watch your food and not let it burn on top or bottom. Simple tin foil wrapped around 3 sticks in the ground can help to divert the wind. Briquettes when they are almost burned up, will start to lose their heat, so be sure to replenish your heat source when needed. The average size briquette lasts at full heat value for 40 to 45 minutes. On the next page I have given you a simple formula for unexpected company. I hope you can enjoy the recipes that follow and will try some of your own.

Camp Chef's new Dutch Dome and Heat Deflector is a welcome addition to cooking with your Dutch Oven on a propane or gas flame.

If You're Cooking on a Volcano,
You'll use Less Briquettes and Cook Faster.
No Mess,
Fewer Briquettes,
Less Chance To Get Burned,
And a Contained Fire.

Seasoning Your Dutch Oven

Well, you just bought your first Dutch Oven and now you're gonna take it home. As you're leaving the store, the salesperson tells you to be sure to season it before you use it. Oh boy, your thinking, what does that mean?

If you ask 100 people how to season a Dutch Oven, you'll probably get 15 different answers. The manufacturers today coat most Dutch Ovens with a protective substance. Usually it is WAX. You will need to heat the oven and burn off the wax. Remove from the fire, and lightly grease it. Put it back on the fire of 30 briquettes in your **VOLCANO** or on your barbecue stove outside.

NEVER CURE THEM IN YOUR HOUSE.

Bake it until it is Black. If the pot appears to be sticky, you have not baked it long or hot enough to burn the oil into the metal. After 1 hour, if it is not black enough, you can let the oven cool down and give it another coat of oil. Return to the heat and bake it more. Be sure to turn the oven upside down so grease does not puddle up in the bottom. I suggest Vegetable oil, Bacon grease, Shortening or Lard.

If your pot is seasoned well and used often, you will find it very easy to clean. Clean your pots while they are hot, they can almost be wiped out with VINEGAR water and virtually no scraping. I mix my Vinegar 1 part Vinegar to 4 parts Water and keep it in a spray bottle in my food box. Vinegar is a great disinfectant and a natural Tenderizer for all foods. Use Natural Apple Cider Vinegar with foods.

Accessorize Your Dutch Oven

Now that you have your Dutch Oven seasoned, have learned how to be a little more safe in its use, and learned how to get the temperature right, there are some other items you will want to have on hand. These will make it easier to cook in your Dutch Oven. So let's make a list of some of the most useful items.

1. Metal scrubbing pad and Matches
2. Hot Pads, Hot Mitts, or Gloves
3. Long Handled Tongs, spoon, fork, knife, and spatula
4. Paper Towels (always keep a roll handy)
5. A small towel or cloth
6. A "Lid Lifter"
7. A "Trivet" (or two)
8. A spray bottle of "Vinegar Water" (see next page)
9. A spray bottle of "Cooking Oil"

As you cook with your Dutch Oven, you will find that you use many of these items every time. You will probably find other items that you love to have on hand and ready for use when desired. You should make up a "Cook Box" or "Possibles Bag" in which you can place all the stuff you use regularly. This way, you won't have to hunt all over when you get the itch to cook up that special dish the family loves so much.

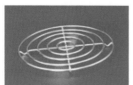

You may be asking yourself about now, "What is a Trivet"?

For those unfamiliar with the term, here are some pictures. They vary in shape and use, but are basically a metal framework on which you can place something in order to keep it over the underlying surface (i.e. so as not to burn your table with a hot Dutch Oven).

Meat trivets work inside a Dutch Oven to keep meat off the bottom.

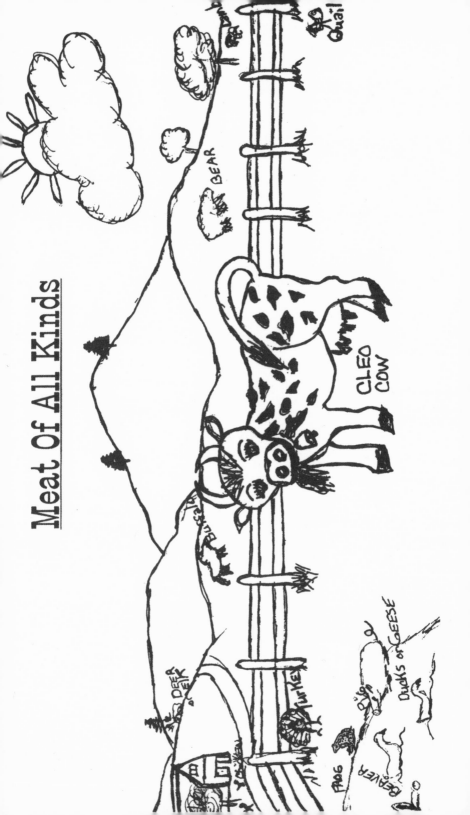

Meat Of All Kinds

Meats and Sauces of all Kinds

Barbecue Sauce for all Meats

1 cup Catsup
1/4 cup Vinegar
2 tbsp. Worcestershire Sauce
1/2 tsp. Liquid Smoke
1/2 or more cup Onions (chopped)
1/2 cup Celery (chopped)
1 cup Tomatoes (chopped)
1/4 cup Green Peppers (optional)

This sauce will work with any meat.

Put all ingredients in a pan or Dutch Oven and simmer until all vegetables are well done. You can add the meat to the sauce and continue to cook until the meat is done, or place the meat in another pan and cover with enough sauce to taste. You can also spice up your leftovers with the sauce by simmering the meat in it to flavor and taste. The longer you simmer the thicker it gets.

Jerky will keep indefinitely and can be made from any animal meat. Elk, Moose, Deer, Beef, Pork, Lamb, Turkey, Chicken. Be sure to trim off all fats.

Old Fashion Deer Jerky

About 3 lbs. Meat, (cut into strips)
1 tbsp. Salt
1 tbsp. Onion Powder or Med Onion Minced
1 tsp. Garlic Powder (1/2 small Garlic)
1/3 cup Worcestershire Sauce
1/4 cup Soy Sauce or Liquid Smoke
2 tbsp. Pepper

Mix all ingredients together and let stand overnight in the refrigerator. The thinner the meat strips the better. Place cut strips in the sauce and let soak for 12 hours. Turning the meat will help it dry faster. Place the meat strips on a drying rack and cover with a cheese cloth or place in the oven on 150 degrees and dry for 8 to 12 hours. You will have to adjust the drying time if the temperature is above or below. Meat should be dry, but have a rubber consistency. If the drying is to long it will become real chewy, which isn't bad if you like to exercise your jaws.

Log Cabin Chicken Pie

2 cups Sifted Flour
1 tsp. Salt
1 Egg
2/3 cups Lard (shortening)
1 tbsp. Lemon Juice (optional)
2 or 3 tbsp. Cold Milk

Sift together flour and salt, cut in lard until particles are as small as peas. Blend together in a separate bowl, egg, lemon juice and toss with flour mix. Add 2 tbsp. of milk and toss with flour until moist enough to form a ball. Do not work flour any more than necessary. Roll out on floured board or pastry cloth and loosely put in 10-inch pie pan.

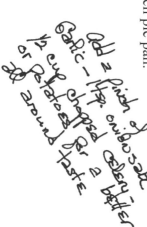

Add 2 pinch of Garlic — 1/4 tsp. onion salt celery 1/2 cup chopped for a better or 3# potatoes around taste.

Filling for Pie

1/2 cup Rich Chicken, Turkey, Beef, or Pork Stock
3 tbsp. Flour (mixed in 1/4 cup water)
3 cups Diced Chicken meat

Heat the Chicken Stock (do not boil). Add Flour to 1/4 cup water and mix to a paste. Add to Chicken Stock, stirring constantly. When thickened, add the 3 cups of Chicken and spoon into pie shell.

Topping for the Pie

Mix 1 1/2 cups Bread Crumbs with 1 medium, finely chopped Onion. Blend in 1/2 tsp. of Salt, Pepper and 1/2 cup of finely chopped Celery. Moisten with 1 to 1 1/2 cups warm Chicken Stock. Spread over the filling and place in oven. Bake hot (375) for 40 minutes.

Prairie Chicken or Sage Grouse

First scald the bird and then skin it. Scalding will keep the feathers from sticking to the bird. Cut apart by joints, and carefully check for buckshot. It takes over 3 weeks to boil the buckshot soft, so be sure to remove it from the bird. Parboil the bird with some onion and drain of water. If it is an old bird, put 1/4 cup vinegar in the water, marinate 2 hours to make the bird tender. After draining, rub the bird with butter or bacon grease. Salt and pepper, broil over fire or roll in flour and fry. Put in a bowl or Dutch Oven and cover to keep warm. Spread a little butter on each piece to keep from drying out. Served with sour dough rolls and currant jelly.

You can substitute Chicken, Turkey, Pheasant or any Fowl.

Put a few grains of Rice in your salt or sugar shaker to keep it from lumping up.

You Wish Chicken Legs

2 cups Ham (cut in large chunks)
2 cups Veal (cut in large chunks)
1/4 cup Milk or a Beaten Egg
1/2 cup Bread or Cracker Crumbs
4 Onions (quartered)

Place chunks of Ham & Veal on skewer alternating with Onion chunks. Salt and Pepper to taste. Roll in Milk or egg mixture and then in crumbs. Fry slowly over a low fire until the meat is brown. Turning often. To make tender, pour 1/4 cup of water in the pan and simmer for 1 hour on low heat. Excellent with greens or potatoes boiled with skins.

Eat your hearts out city fellows, we keep the real chickens for the eggs.

These recipes date back to the 1700's!

Mulligan Stew
from the Old Country

Any leftover Meat
Any leftover Vegetables
Any leftover Juice from Roasts or Stews or Gravies

When out camping or at home, most people save the leftovers. That is where the Mulligan stew originated. Pour all the juices and gravies in a pot. Simmer together and season if needed. Cut the fats from meats, any and all kinds that you have and cut into small pieces in the juices. Simmer for 30 minutes. Add all the vegetables that are available as leftovers or canned. Potatoes, celery, corn, carrots, turnips, parsley, beans, onions, parsnips, tomatoes, etc. Cover and let simmer. Time depends on whether the vegetables were cooked or raw. Add a few spices if you desire. Garlic, thyme, basil or sage. Whatever trips your trigger.

Stewed Chicken

1 rather plump Chicken
2 stocks of Celery
2 slices of Onion
1 tbsp. Salt
Pepper to taste

Dress, clean and cut up chicken at the joints. Put in pan deep enough to cover the bird. If the chicken is old and tough, be sure to soak in enough water to cover the bird and add 1/4 cup vinegar. This will make the bird as tender as a spring chicken. After soaking 2 or 3 hours, drain off water and recover with fresh water. Add Celery and Onions. Add salt. Simmer for 1 to 1 1/2 hours. Add potatoes, carrots, celery, peas, if desired and cook until tender. Thicken gravy if you wish. Serve warm. Makes an excellent late supper, with homemade bread. Be sure to discard the water.

A dash of parsley
Garlic help the flavor

Cooking is an art.
The better you are, the more company you draw.

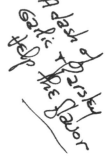

Wild Game Birds

Most wild birds are better if Parboiled in onion and salt water. Add 1/4 cup Apple Cider Vinegar to salt water.

Doves: Clean and skin. Parboil, roast over campfire or fry in hot oil. Baked with sage dressing or corn bread stuffing.

Dove Pie: Cut up carrots, celery, onions, green pepper, turnips or potatoes in Dutch Oven. Salt and pepper to taste, add parboiled dove meat, cover with sourdough biscuits and bake.

Quail, Sage Hen, Grouse, Pheasants & Quail can be cooked the same way. Cornish game also.

Substitute Chicken for Wild Fowl.

Apple Stuffing for Birds

Wash apples well and remove any blemishes or worm holes. Cut into pieces and remove seeds. Place inside of bird and bake as usual.

Sage Dressing by Granny

Add parsley a touch or Dot leaves of cumin of variety

4 cups Dried Bread Crumbs
4 Eggs
1 large Onion
1 cup Celery, chopped
2 tbsp. Sage
1 tsp. Salt
2 tsp. Pepper
1/4 cup Thyme (optional)

With enough water to moisten all ingredients. Combine all ingredients chopped up fine in a large bowl. Put the dressing in or around the bird. Double the recipe for larger portions.

Turkey - Wild or Tame - Goose

Clean bird thoroughly. Rub inside with salt and pepper. Stuff with sage dressing or apple dressing. Birds can be roasted in the Dutch Oven or in regular stove oven.

Wild Game Jerky

1 lb. Wild Meat
1 qt. Water
1/2 cup Salt
1 tbsp. Pepper
1/4 cup Sugar

Cut meat with the grain in very thin strips and as long as possible. Soak in solution of above mixture for 24 hours. **Do not use aluminum pans.** After washing the meat, dry for 1 to 2 hours in the air. If you do not have a smoker, rub meat with liquid smoke and dry in food dryer.

a little worcheschire sauce is a good additive

Venison

Remember that venison can be a lot like Mutton. Be sure to warm the dish before serving.

Roast Leg

Wash meat thoroughly, sprinkle salt and pepper all over and roll in flour. Wrap leg with salt pork or bacon. Be sure that fat is mostly cut away. Roast uncovered in moderately warm oven (300). Approximately 25 minutes per pound. Be sure roast is served warm.

No man really knows what he believes in until he starts to raise his own children.

Buffalo Company Soup
For _lots_ (and lots) of company

1 Buffalo
2 sacks Onions
2 sacks Carrots
1 lg. sack Flour
1 box Salt
1 box Pepper
2 Rabbits (optional)

This recipe should feed about 2,000 people. Approximately one week before the company arrives, begin cutting the meat into small pieces. This could take 3 or 4 days. You should get extra help, because your arms and fingers get quite tired. Now place in a large container and add enough water to cover. Brown the flour in buffalo grease (fat) that is scraped from the hide. Pour into meat mixture. Simmer for 3 or 4 days. Add veggies and cook till soft. If extra people show up, add the 2 rabbits to the pot. But remember, don't add them if you don't need them. Most people don't like hare in their soup.

Jackrabbit Stew
Another delicious company dish

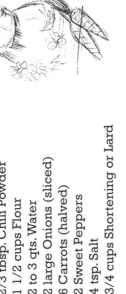

2 Rabbits (or 3 Chickens)
1 large Onion (chopped)
1 tsp. Salt
2/3 tbsp. Chili Powder
1 1/2 cups Flour
2 to 3 qts. Water
2 large Onions (sliced)
6 Carrots (halved)
2 Sweet Peppers
4 tsp. Salt
3/4 cups Shortening or Lard

Cut meat into serving size pieces. Roll in flour, and brown in oil in frying pan. Drain off excess oil, and return meat to pan. Use chopped onion to fry meat and sliced in the stew. Add water to meat and simmer for two hours. Add all vegetables and simmer until carrots are tender. The company won't mind the hare in this soup, but they may object to the feathers.

Bear Meat may be substituted

Cowboy Stew

1 lb. Stew Meat
1 cup Beans (best if soaked overnight)
1 cup Tomatoes or Tomato Juice
1 Onion (finely chopped)
Salt & Pepper to taste
1/2 cup Celery
2 oz. Side Pork or Bacon (3 strips)

Be sure to wash and soak beans overnight, this will help shorten cooking time. Cook pork until fat is fried out and crisp. Remove pork from pan. Lightly flour chunks of meat (Buffalo, Elk, Deer, Beef, Bear, etc.) and fry until brown. Add Beans, Tomatoes and Seasoning. Be sure to put pork back in stew. Cover and cook for 2 to 3 hours. If you add 1/2 cup water, dumplings can be put on top 20 minutes before serving.

"Partner; it's eatin' worth this one."

Never Fail Dumplings

2 cups Flour (sifted)
1/2 tsp. Salt
4 level tsp. Baking Powder
1 Egg
Milk, enough to fill cup when egg is beaten

Sift together dry ingredients. In a measuring cup, break the egg. With fork, beat lightly and fill cup to top with Milk. Add dry ingredients and mix enough to moisten dry ingredients. Let stand for 5 minutes to rise. Drop batter by spoonfuls onto stew. Cover and cook for 20 minutes. These are just as good warmed the next day.

Add a little Extra salt if you like a more robust Dumpling

Dip your spoon in hot water before dropping dumplings or measuring shortening. This will make the batter or shortening drop off easier.

Squeak Bubble and Meat

Boil head of Cabbage in salt water and drain. Chop into small pieces and put into bowl. Meanwhile, in fry pan, cut cold, already cooked meat in pieces, salt pepper and fry them. Drain off fat from frying. Add a little butter to meat, put Cabbage in fry pan. Add a little Pepper and gently stir to equally cook cabbage and meat. When ready, remove from fire and add a few drops of vinegar.

'Apple Cider Vinegar Preferred'

Making Corn Beef

In a cool place, place 3 lbs. of beef, venison, elk, or moose, in a Crockpot with 1/2 cup salt, 1/4 cup vinegar and water to cover. Leave for 10 to 12 days. Put the meat in a sauce pan with cold water. Bring to boil, skim occasionally and then place on fire. Simmer slowly for several house or until meat is thoroughly cooked. Blanch separately 2 heads of cabbage and remove the centers. About 1 hour before the meat is done, put in with meat. If too salty to the taste, put in a peeled potato and remove when soft. This will pull out the salt. Drain and arrange on dish with parsley. You can add 1/2 cup shredded Carrots to sweeten the taste.

To remove the salty taste from any cooked dish, simply put in a raw peeled potato and remove when cooked. This will absorb most of the salt taste. You can also add 1/2 cup shredded Carrots.

Bay leaves or a pinch of Nutmeg will give will meat a secret flavor.

Country Pot Roast

5 to 6 lb. Pot Roast (any meat)
1/4 cup Oil or Bacon Fat
3 cups Water
1/2 tsp. Pepper
1 tsp. Salt
1 cup Flour
Potatoes
Carrots
1 Onion

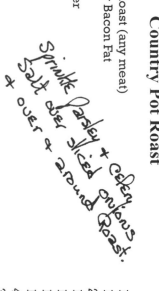

Sprinkle Parsley + Celery Salt over sliced onions + over + around Roast.

Brown or sear meat in Dutch Oven or roaster pan in the oil. Add water and seasonings. Cover and cook for 2 hours at 300 degrees. Drain off juice in a separate pan. Leave about 2 tbsp. of juice on the roast. Put in the vegetables and return to fire. Set juice aside with enough water added to make 3 cups. Make paste with water and flour. When veggies are done, add flour to juice and simmer until thick. Add salt and pepper to taste. Gravy can be made in the Dutch Oven or roaster pan if desired.

Sheepherder Leftover Pie

1 1/2 cups Celery
1/2 cup Water
2 cups leftover Gravy (1 gravy packet 2 cups water)
1 tsp. Salt
1/2 Onion (chopped)
1/4 tsp. Salt
1/4 tsp. Paprika
4 cups leftover Roast
3 separated Eggs
3 cups mashed Potatoes

Great way yet. to use up left. over Roast

Cook celery & onion in water until tender. Combine with beef and 1 cup gravy. Add 1 tsp. salt and place in hot oven. Beat egg yolks and add to mashed potatoes. Combine egg whites and 1/4 tsp. salt. Beat until peaks form. Fold this mixture into potatoes and spread over the meat mixture. Sprinkle with paprika and parsley if desired and bake until light brown. 20 minutes in 375 to 400 degree oven. Serve with remaining hot gravy. Great with ranch rolls.

Always save leftover gravies to enhance other dishes. Extra good to serve with hot rolls.

Short-ribs and Dumplings

3 lbs. Beef Short-ribs
1 med. Onion
3 tbsp. Lard (or substitute)
3 cups Water
1/4 cup Flour
1 tbsp. Salt
1/8 tsp. Pepper
2 cups sliced Carrots
1/4 cup chopped Celery

Sprinkle flour, salt and pepper over the cut ribs. Put lard and Onion in a large skillet. Add the meat and brown lightly. Add the water and cover. Simmer for 1/2 hour until tender. Top with dumplings that have 1/4 cup parsley added to the mixture, baking powder biscuits can be used. Excellent in Dutch Oven while camping, or at home.

VARIATIONS;
• Almost any vegetable can be added to the meat for the last 30 minutes of cooking to balance the meal.

Mrs. Hales Requested Meat Loaf

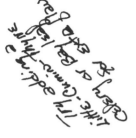

1 lb. Hamburger (4 cups)
1/4 lb. Sausage (1 cup)
3 Eggs
2 cups Bread Crumbs (corn flakes works well)
1 med. Onion & Green Pepper (finely chopped)
1 cup celery (finely chopped)
2 tsp. Salt
1/2 tsp. Pepper
1 cup Tomato Sauce or Canned Tomato (optional)

Mix all ingredients together and place in loaf pan to bake at about 350 degrees for 1 hour. Top can be brushed with tomato sauce. 2 loaf pans.

VARIATIONS;
• Add a pinch of one of the following; thyme, allspice, cumin, sage, parsley or 1 tsp. garlic.
• Or add; 1 cup cooked rice, crushed corn flakes, oatmeal, cracker crumbs, mashed potatoes, grated carrots, turnips or parsnips. 1 can kernel corn.

Mincemeat for Every Use

3 lb. Boiled Neck Meat (Venison, Buffalo or Beef)
1 lb. Suet (Lard)
3 lb. Sugar
1/2 peck Apples
2 lbs. Raisins
1 1/2 lbs. Currents
2 or 3 cups Dried Fruit
1 tbsp. Nutmeg
5 cents of Powdered Mace, Allspice and Cinnamon to suit taste (2 tsp. each)

Chop the meat, dried fruit, apples and lard very fine. Add seasonings, pour enough sweet cider vinegar over mixture to make a thick batter, warm thoroughly. Allow to cool. Cover and use as needed for cookies, dressing, cakes or pies.

This is Great cookie fillings

How to Boil Water:
Place water in pot over fire, cover; water is ready when bubbles form. Remember not to burn water, this may make your food taste funny.

Dutch Oven Baked Beans

1 small bag of Beans (1 qt. Beans)
1 hand full Onions (chopped) (1/3 cup)
1/2 lb. Salt Pork (10 strips Bacon)
1 lg. pinch of Salt (1 tsp.)
leaves off Mustard Weed (1 tsp.)
4 tbsp. Molasses

Beans are best soaked overnight in cold water. Simmer in oven till tender. Place all ingredients in Dutch Oven, cover and bake. You may add tomatoes if available.

Mouth watering add 1 cup crushed pineapple.

CHOPPING ONIONS WITHOUT TEARS
- Cut the root end off last.
- Chill before chopping.
- Peel under cold water.
- Rinse hands in cool water often while peeling.
- Spray with vinegar water solution.

Chili from Way Back

2 lbs. chopped Meat (any kind)
2 Onions (chopped up fine)
2 tsp. Salt
2 tbsp. Chili Powder
5 cups Beans (soaked overnight) or canned
3 or 4 Tomatoes (if available) or Diced Canned Tomatoes
Pepper to taste

Roll meat in flour and brown in a deep, heavy skillet with onions. Add rest of ingredients and let simmer until soupy. Excellent served with sourdough rolls or cornbread.

Did you know that canned beans have less gas than fresh soaked beans.

Chili Greens

Wash young tender dandelions, cut into strips. Put into bowl. Fry 4 or 5 strips of salt pork to a crisp stage. Cut up and pour over greens. Spoon a small amount of chili over greens and serve.

Wild Violets

Vitamin A and C are very important to the system. When in the out of doors, eat 1/2 cup violet leaf greens for the required daily amount. Great for people with colds too.

When soup or meat is cooking and there seems to be too much grease, drop a cold leaf of lettuce in the pot.

It will absorb the grease. Remove and throw away.

Chili Wheat

Soak the wheat overnight before you plan on cooking it. Put 2 cups of wheat in 4 cups of water. Drain before adding to recipe.

2 cups Wheat (soaked and cleaned)
2 lbs. Meat (any kind)
1 heaping tsp. of Chili Powder
1 Garlic (mashed fine)
Salt and Pepper to taste
2 large Onions (cut up)
4 or 5 Tomatoes (if available)
    or Tomato Juice

Mix tomato juice and wheat in Dutch Oven, cook over low heat for 3 or 4 hours. Cook remaining ingredients in fry pan. Simmer for 30 minutes in with wheat. Remove and serve with hot baked bread or corn bread. Homemade crackers can be used also.

This recipe will help you learn to use your wheat.

When you are creaming butter and sugar together, rinse the bowl in hot water. They will cream together faster.

Sweet Crackers (1720)
(This is a real old recipe)

1/2 cup Lard or Shortening
1/2 cup Fresh Butter
3 cups Sugar
2 med. Eggs (room temperature)
1 pt. Sweet Milk - 2 cups
*Baking Ammonia 10 cents worth
*Lemon Oil 10 cents worth
Flour to roll on

Cream shortening & Sugar, blend well with Eggs. Add ammonia (baking soda 2 tsp.) to milk, this will make the Milk foam. Stir in flour & milk mixture alternately with cream mixture. Make a moderately stiff dough.

Pound dough 1/2 hour after mixing.

Roll dough rather thick & place on cookie sheet or jelly roll pan. Cut in squares & prick with fork. Bake until golden brown in 375 degree oven.

• Baking Ammonia is the same as soda.
• Lemon oil can be substituted with any cooking oil.

This is a fun recipe to try with your kids.

Pork & Sweet Potato Pie

3 cups Pork
2 cups Water
6 tbsp. Flour
1 tbsp. Salt
1/2 tsp. Pepper
1/4 cup cold Water
2 cups cooked Sweet Potatoes (diced)
1 cup cooked Peas
1 cup Onions (diced)
1 1/2 cup cooked Carrots (diced)

Cube pork, flour and brown in 2 tablespoons of lard. Add water and simmer for 1/2 hour or until tender. Blend fry ingredients and mix with water until smooth. Add vegetables and cook in oven baking dish. Cover with onion biscuits, bake 20 minutes in hot oven.

Insert a clean nail in a potato for baking,

to help shorten the baking time.

Onion Biscuits

1 1/2 cups Flour
1/2 tsp. Salt
1/3 cup Lard
2 tsp. Baking Powder
1/2 cup Dried Onions
2/3 cup Milk

Sift or toss together dry ingredients, cut in lard or shortening. Mixture should resemble coarse meal or small peas. Blend in onions, mix in milk until flour is dampened. Knead gently on floured board. Roll out and cut into pieces. Place biscuits on top of hot meat. Bake in hot oven 425 degrees.

Delicious

Porky's Pie Crust

Sift together; 1 1/2 cups flour, 1/4 tsp. salt, 1/4 tsp. baking powder.

Measure and cut in; 1/2 cup lard or shortening.

Mixture should be like coarse corn meal. Moisten with 1/4 cup cold water stirring with a knife or fork only until the flour mixture holds together as a ball. Roll out on floured board to 1/4 inch thick. Makes a 2 crust pie or 10 or 12 possible.

Hot Water Pie Crust

Stir hot water and lard in equal amounts. This will become foamy and somewhat creamy. Add 1/2 tsp. salt and 3 times the amount of flour. It will roll very well while it is still hot. Makes tender flaky crust and will keep for several days.

Meat Pie Possibles

1 cup raw Potatoes
4 tbsp. Onions (finely chopped)
1 cup Cooked Meat (any kind)

Add 1 cup Celery chopped for flavor

Chop and mix all ingredients together. Salt and pepper to taste. Set aside. Make pie dough, roll out and cut in rectangular pieces. Moisten the edges and place a big helping on the dough. Put 2nd square over the meat mix and press edges together. After sealing the edges well, prick the top with a fork or knife to allow the steam to escape. Place on sheet and bake 45 minutes in moderate oven (350). These are so good that you probably will not get to taste how good they are cold.

This is wonderful on Biscuits or served on Bread or Toast with the Gravy on Top.

The less you work with pie crust, the flakier it will be.

Skillet Pork Chops

3 tbsp. Flour	1 tbsp. Oil
5 tbsp. Parmesan Cheese (divided)	2 medium Onions (sliced)
	1/3 cup Water
1 1/2 tsp. Salt	3 medium Zucchini (sliced)
1/2 tsp. Pepper	1/2 tsp. Paprika
1/2 tsp. Dill Weed	
6 or 7 Pork Chops	

In a large plastic bag, combine flour and 2 tablespoons Parmesan cheese, salt, pepper, and dill weed. Place pork chops in bag and shake to coat. Shake off excess flour in bag and preserve. Heat oil in a skillet over medium heat; fry and brown pork chops on both sides. Reduce heat; place onion slices on chops. Add water to skillet, cover, and simmer for 15 minutes. Place zucchini slices over onion slices. Mix remaining Parmesan cheese with preserved flour in bag; sprinkle over zucchini, put paprika over that and simmer for 25 minutes or until chops are nice and tender. Excellent served over rice.

Catalina Island Chicken

2 (8 ounce) bottles of Catalina Dressing (or French)
1 (12 ounce) bottle Apricot Jam
1 pkg. Instant Onion Soup Mix
8 Chicken Breasts (skinless)

Mix dressing, jam, and soup mix and pour over chicken. Bake in 12-inch Dutch Oven at 350 degrees oven for about 1 1/2 hours. For 350 degree oven, use 10-12 briquettes on bottom and 15-16 on top. Replenish your briquettes as needed to maintain the 350 degree temperature.

When pan frying or sauteing, be sure to heat the pan first and melt butter or shortening. This will keep the vegetable or meat from sticking.

Buffalo – The Meat of the Indians

The Indians relied on the meat of the buffalo to keep them thru the winter months. They made a jerky out of it by adding fruits and berries. The meat was first dried in thin small strips in the sun. Sometimes they would smoke it over a fire to hasten the drying time. This usually makes the meat sweeter. The meat is then chopped to a fine powder or ground with the rock. Dried fruits or berries were then mashed in with the meat. The meat mixture was then put in leather bags and hot melted fat poured over the top. The bag was sewn shut and put away for winter. This was a very tasty treat in the winter and could be eaten plain, made into soup, fried or roasted over the camp fire. The Indians depended on this for survival. The name given to this was Plemican or pemmican.

"BUFFALO"

Buffalo is a very rich red meat. Sometimes sweet to the taste. It can also be tough at times so soaking it in a vinegar solution will tenderize it. (1/4 c. vinegar to 3/4 c. water). This goes for steaks and roasts and chops. Soak one hour and dry steak. Then roll in flour and fry in lard or shortening.

Roasts; soak, then drain and place in oven to bake. Season with salt and pepper and a touch of onion.

Buffalo may be purchased in California and refuges in Cody, Wyo. and Southwest Oklahoma.

Show me a home where the Buffalo roam, and I'll show you a home with problems.

Page: 34

Baked Woodchuck

Prepare by cleaning the animal thoroughly and removing all the excess fat. Be sure to remove the gland high on the inside of the fore-legs. It is about bean size. There is also one on the back bone just in front of the hip-bone. Season with salt and pepper. Roll in flour, put in Dutch Oven and cover with water. Simmer until the water is gone. Sprinkle with garlic, put apple dressing around bird, bake for 30 to 35 minutes. Will melt in your mouth.

Southern Chestnut Dressing

Using basic apple stuffing, substitute one pound (3 cups) of cooked, finely chopped chestnuts, for grated fruit rind. This can add the old fashion flavor of the south to your wild birds.

Apple Dressing for Birds

2 or 3 cups Bread Crumbs
2 Eggs
1 small Onion
2 medium Apples (diced)
3 slices Bacon (chopped fine)
A pinch of Thyme
Salt and Pepper to taste
2 tbsp. Grated Orange Rind (optional)
1 tbsp. Grated Lemon Rind (optional)

This is a very tasty dressing. Combine all ingredients and stuff the bird or bake separately for 30 minutes. The grated rind gives it a citrus taste that is hard to beat. This is extra good in wild or tame birds. Also, with roast pork or beef.

If birds are old, parboil with 1/4 cup of vinegar in the water, discard after use. This will tenderize the bird.

Also, baking soda in the water will do the same thing. Only a small amount, 1/2 tsp. or less.

Wagon Wheel Beans

2 cups Beans (soaked overnight)
1 large Onion
1/4 lb. Sliced Salt Pork (or Bacon)

After beans have soaked overnight, drain and wash them. Add onion and pork. Simmer for 2 to 3 hours. Add water as needed to keep covered. Serve with corn bread or fried bread. This is easy eatin.

*This was a Recipe
Started beau Recipe
for chuck wagons*

*"While soaking beans, place a tbsp. of
vinegar in the water to remove gases.
A tsp. of soda will also work.*

Fried Rabbit

2 Young Rabbits (or other Meat)
3 cups Milk
1 tsp. Salt
2 Egg Yolks
1 1/4 cups Flour
1/2 cup Fat (Shortening or Bacon Grease)
1 tbsp. Parsley (optional, but good)

mm-mm-good

Wash, dress and cut up rabbit. Combine Egg Yolks, 1 cup Milk, and 1 cup Flour. Beat until smooth, add Salt. Dip rabbit in batter and fry in fat until brown. Reduce heat & cook till tender. Use milk to make gravy. Stirring constantly till thick. Pour over rabbit and serve warm. Delicious.

*"Money can't buy happiness, but it
makes misery a lot more comfortable.*

Bear Meat

Bear meat is quite rich and sweet. This is great for making into patties and frying slow until brown. Fry with onions or mushrooms or bacon. Sometimes the meat is dry and requires extra lard or shortening. Bear can be cooked any way that you do beef, elk, buffalo, antelope or venison. The Indians really liked this meat for its flavor. If the bear was really old, the more you chewed the meat, the bigger it got and therefore lasted all winter. Dutch ovens cook them best.

Dumplings

1 cup Flour
1/4 tsp. Salt
2 tsp. Baking Powder
1 Egg

Mix dry ingredients, add beaten egg & enough water to make a soft dough. Roll on floured board and cut into squares. Place on top of stews the last 20 minutes to be cooked. Do not remove cover of pot while dumplings are cooking.

Mountaineer Stew

your home grown veggies are best.

2 1/2 lbs. Meat
2 1/2 cups Water
1 tsp. Salt
1/2 tsp. Pepper
1/2 cup Greens (Onions)
3 or 4 Carrots
3 or 4 Sego Lily Bulbs (Potatoes Substitute)
2 cups wild Vegetables (or store bought)
3 tbsp. Flour and 1/4 cup Water

Cut meat in small pieces. Add water and spices. Cover Dutch Oven and simmer for 1 1/2 hours, stir occasionally. Add all the rest of ingredients and simmer till tender. Mix flour and water together and make paste. Add to stew. By changing meat to lamb and adding peas the last 15 minutes, this becomes Irish Mountain Stew.

Vinegar is a meat cooks best friend.

Fried Woodchuck

Clean bird as for baking. If old be sure to parboil. This will also help to take off all the fat. Cut meat into strips, roll in egg and corn meal. Fry in bacon fat until tender and brown.

Ground Hog or Beaver

The broad tail of the beaver is the best part. Clean wild animals very carefully. Parboil in salt and onion water for one hour. Sear on both sides and place in Dutch Oven. Season to taste and Apple dressing may be placed around tail. Ground Hog may be cut up and fried and placed in dressing. Bake for 30 minutes at 350 degrees.

Opossum or Raccoon

Young Opossum or Raccoon is the best. Be sure to parboil them with onion, salt and Bay leaf. These animals are excellent eating with Sweet Potato Pie or sweet potatoes baked around them.

Squirrel Soup

Clean, wash and quarter 3 or 4 good size squirrels. Simmer in pot on the back of the stove totally covered with water. Add a tablespoon of salt and cook until the meat is in shreds. Strain thru colander to get rid of little unwanted bones. Return to pot, thicken with flour. Add carrots, celery and parsley leaves. Toast 2 slices of bread, refry them in butter. Pour hot soup over toast. Very, very good.

Pork or Beef can be substituted, Chicken or Turkey will work also.

Rattlesnake Stew

1 Rattlesnake (medium size)
1 tsp. Salt (more if needed)
2 or 3 shakes of Pepper
5 Sego Lily Bulb's (potatoes)
3 or 4 Wild Onions
Celery, Garlic and Carrots (optional)

Very carefully catch one medium size snake being careful not to get bitten. Remove head and tail, skin and clean the snake. Cut into small pieces, flour and fry in bacon grease or lard. Add all seasonings and cover with water in pot to boil. Simmer for 1 hour and add more water if necessary. Add the vegetables and simmer until vegetables are done. This is a very tasty dish, and will resemble the taste of chicken. Rattlesnake meat can sometimes be purchased in specialty food stores.

Fried Rattlesnake Meat

Younger snakes are the best for tenderness. After cleaning the meat, it can be rolled in flour and fried. Season lightly and eat. For a variety, it can be rolled in a flour & egg mixture. Then dipped in bread or cracker crumbs and fried. Bacon grease is an excellent addition to the meat. Secured to a stick and roasted over the open camp fire is also very good.

Seasonings to use are; Onion, Garlic, Salt, Pepper, Celery and Cumin.

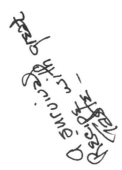

Wooden spoons should be disinfected periodically, soak 1 tbsp. Vinegar, 1 cup water.

Fish

Fish should be thoroughly cooked, whatever variety. Salmon and Mackerel can be boiled and does not affect their flavor. Lemon can reduce the oily taste of most fish.

Carp

Carp is the fish mostly eaten in the Northern states, due to the cold waters, is fresh and firm. Warm waters give it a muddy taste and mushy texture. After thoroughly cleaning the fish, let it stand in 1/4 cup vinegar water for an hour. Make a good bread dressing, some prefer corn bread, and stuff the fish. You may want to tie the fish together or sew it to keep dressing in place. Then mix parsley, bacon bits, onions, carrots & celery together in oil and spread on fish. Baste throughout the cooking period. Don't get the oven to hot, it will burn and dry the vegetables. A 1 or 2 lb. fish should cook about 1 1/2 hours. Highly seasoned tomato sauce or Barbeque sauce goes well with this fish.

Fish Dressing

2 cups Dry Bread Crumbs
1/4 cup Butter (melted) (or Bacon Grease)
1/2 cup Salt
A pinch of Pepper
1 Onion
A pinch of Parsley
1 tbsp. Chopped Pickles

Mix all ingredients together and add enough water to pack together. Sometimes an egg or two will help hold the dressing together. This will work for all kinds of fish.

Moisten a paper towel or cloth with vanilla and place in refrigerator. Good for removing smells.

Catfish

There are approximately 36 different varieties of catfish. Mud cat, Bull head, Yellow cat, Blue cat, Flannel mouth and various other names. The most popular of the cat fish is the Channel Catfish. These come in a variety of sizes. This fish can get huge in size, sometimes caught at over 30 lbs. This is a very easy fish to clean. Then you skin and wash and it's ready for the oven, or fry pan. The only bone to worry about is the back bone. In the South, this fish is dipped in batter and rolled in cornmeal and fried. Then salt & peppered and served with hot cakes, cornbread or fried okra, it is positively delicious. It can be baked with dressing, rolled in flour and fried, dipped and deep fried or saved for leftovers and made into fishcakes.

A small bowl of charcoal (the kind used for houseplants) will eliminate odors in your refrigerator. This absorbs very fast. Baking soda also works.

Fish Cakes

These cakes can be made from any leftover fish, whether it is fresh, frozen or canned. The fish will need to be mashed into shreds. Approximately 1 cup of fish, to 1 cup of Flour or Breadcrumbs. Toss with a fork, and add a well beaten egg. This will hold the mixture together. Season with Salt, Pepper, Onion, or Garlic. Thyme, Curry, Marjoram or Tarragon can be added also. Just a pinch for flavor. Then fry over a medium fire.

Soaking potatoes in salt water for 20 minutes before baking will make them bake faster.

Frog Legs – Jumpin Gimminy

The legs are the only part of the frog that is usually eaten. The longer the hind legs, the better. These are considered a real specialty dish. The meat is tender and white. Will have the consistency of a chicken. They can be broiled or fried. A squeeze of lemon or a side of mayonnaise makes the dish complete. Two large legs will usually satisfy the average appetite. Frog legs are full of protein and vitamin B. When frying, lightly flour and salt. Boiling or broiling can be done as suggested.

Rejuvenate old lemons, by placing them in hot water and bringing to the boiling point.

Leave in water for 5 minutes but turn off the heat. Then cool and refrigerate.

Potato Cakes with Vegetables

Make Mashed Potatoes per recipe

6 cups Mashed Potatoes
6 tbsp. Butter
2 whole Eggs
Salt and Pepper to taste
1/8 tsp. Nutmeg (optional)
3 cups Vegetables (cooked)
1 Egg (beaten)

Mix mashed potatoes with butter, whole eggs, salt, pepper and nutmeg. Make into 16 balls and allow to cool. Flatten into thick round patties. Place on a greased baking sheet. Put 1/2 cup vegetables in center of the patty and cover with 2nd patty. Brush top of each patty with beaten egg. Bake for 15 to 20 minutes at 375 degrees. Serves 8.

Stuffed Turnips

Wash and par-boil 6 turnips of the same size. When they are tender, cut into thin slice from their top and spoon out the inside. This will create a well inside. You can fill these with sage dressing that you would use for chicken or turkey. These may also be stuffed with a meat loaf mixture. Put a slice of onion on top and bake. 350 degrees for 25 to 30 minutes. Baste with some melted butter or bacon grease.

Turnip Cups

Prepare the turnips as above and fill with warm creamed vegetables or creamed meats.

Sautéed Turnips

Prepare as before. Cut into small chunks. Sauté in butter with a small green onion and some mushrooms. Season with salt and pepper and a dash of garlic.

Dutch Oven Baked Beans

3/4 lb. Bacon (fried and grease removed)
1 lb. Ground Beef
1 Onion (chopped)
1 can Kidney Beans (large)
1 can Buttered Lima Beans
1 can Pork and Beans
1 cup Brown Sugar
1 tbsp Vinegar
1 tbsp Liquid Smoke
1 cup Ketchup

Brown the beef & bacon with the onion and pour off most of the grease. Add bacon, all beans and the other ingredients. Simmer in the Dutch Oven for 1 1/2 to 2 hours. The taste will simply tingle your taste buds.

To prevent bacon from curling, dip in cold water before frying.

Remember to put salt in pan before heating to help prevent splattering.

Pope Bailey's Jambalaya

1 lb. Pork Pieces
1 lb. Bacon
1 cup Chopped White Fish
1 cup Boneless Chicken (cut up)
1 lb. Smoked Sausage Rolls (sliced)
1 cup Ham Pieces
1 cup Chopped Green Onions
1 cup Chopped Celery
1 each Red & Green Pepper (chopped)
1 cup Diced Tomatoes (fresh or canned)
1 tbsp. (or less) Cajun Seasoning
1 tbsp. Garlic Pepper
1 can Tomato Puree (or 1/2 cup Catsup)
2 cups Uncooked Rice
2 or 3 cups Chicken Broth

Fry bacon in the bottom of a 12" Dutch Oven and add all the meats. Simmer until the meats are cooked through. Cover and allow to simmer slowly until the meats are tender. 30 to 45 minutes. Add all the remaining ingredients and cover. Let the mixture simmer until you can smell it or approximately another 30 minutes.

Fried Turnips

Wash and clean turnips. Cut into strips and remove woody centers if needed. Dip in beaten egg and roll in cracker or bread crumbs. Season with salt, pepper, onion salt, and a touch of garlic. You can fry in bacon grease or oil, and with mushrooms. Fry only till tender. This is an excellent side dish or veggie.

The best Jambalaya will simmer on the stove all day long. Real Jambalaya is mildly spicy and thick. It always has 3 or more meats in the soup mixture.

Fish and Turtle are the most common in the South. Any kind of vegetables can be used including Cabbage, Kohl Robi, Turnips and Sweet Potatoes or Yams.

Hints About Chicken

- Purchase chicken on sale when you can: Whole chickens wrapped well can be frozen for up to a year. Cut-up chickens can be frozen up to 9 months. Giblets should not be frozen over 3 months.

- Refrigerate chicken as soon as you get it home. Poultry can be stored in the coldest part of the refrigerator for up to 2 days.

- Wash Poultry under cold water before cooking. I always add a little cider vinegar to the water to assure it's disinfected. Poultry can carry the salmonella bacteria and that can be destroyed by vinegar and cooking to well done. Juices should be clear, not pink.

- Bacteria can be transferred to counter tops and cutting boards. So wash thoroughly with hot soapy water and wipe with vinegar full strength to assure cleanliness.

- Always thaw poultry in the refrigerator or cold water.

- Refrigerate leftovers promptly. Store gravies and dressings separate.

- Leftover poultry should be eaten in 3 to 4 days or frozen and reheated later.

- Old fashion fried or baked chicken are two of the easiest dishes to prepare.

Wasp Spray is better in the back woods than bear spray. Shoots farther + faster + much easier to get your target.

Soapsuds are a Fantastic Insecticide. Spray them on your Garden Often.

If a Bee or Wasp gets in the House, grab the Hair Spray. It will stiffen their wings immediately. Works on all winged insects.

Baking a Chicken

1 4 to 6 lb. Chicken
1 medium Onion (sliced)
2 tbsp. Log Cabin Seasoning
Spray Bottle of Vinegar Water

Completely thaw bird and place in baking dish on a trivet. This will keep meat out of the dripping and fats. If you are using a 12" deep Dutch Oven, preheat your oven. Spray bird with vinegar water inside and out. Place onion slices around and inside the bird. Sprinkle with seasoning and cover. Bake in regular oven for 1 and 1/2 hours. In Dutch Oven in a Volcano Stove, use 10 charcoal and check for doneness after 50 minutes. Do not raise lid. Bird legs will pull off and away easily when it is done. You will be able to see clear liquid if it's done.

Log Cabin Chicken Soup

Leave dripping from baked chicken in baking dish or Dutch Oven. Add 1 quart of water and let simmer. Cut up 3 carrots (washed well) and 3 stocks of celery. Place in chicken broth. Add 1 tsp. salt, 1/2 tsp. pepper and 1/2 tsp. garlic powder or salt. Bring to a boil and add 1 cup leftover cut up chicken.

Simmer until veggies are tender. Add 2 cups noodles and simmer till done.

You can add some of the chicken meat if you want meat in your soup. Makes a great meal for late supper snacks or an appetizer for a big dinner. Variations can include potatoes, turnips, dumplings, or any other thing you want to experiment with.

To make sure your clothes rinse soap free,
Add 1 cup White Vinegar to final rinse.

Chicken or Turkey Hash

1 cup Leftover White Gravy
1 cup (or more) Leftover Meat
1/2 to 1 cup Leftover Grated Potatoes
1/2 cup Water
1/2 tsp. Salt and Pepper
1/2 tsp. Garlic and Celery Sauce

Put all ingredients into sauce pan and warm up. Serve over toast or biscuits. Sprinkle on parsley flakes for color or decoration. Serve with green salad or vegetables for colorful plate.

Turkey Noodle Casserole

My Favorite

2 cups Chopped Meat (Turkey or Chicken)
2 cups Cooked Noodles
1 Egg
1 cup Milk (mixed with Egg)
1 tbsp. Butter
1/2 cup Celery and Carrots (chopped)
1 med. Onion (chopped)
1/2 cup Bread Crumbs

In a baking dish or 12" Dutch Oven, put alternate layers of meat, noodles, celery, carrots and onions. Be sure to warm and grease Dutch Oven first. End with noodles on top. Sprinkle bread crumbs over noodles. Pour milk/egg mixture over top and dot with butter. Bake for 30 minutes.

To give biscuits or Dumplings a different taste add a Pinch of Mustard or thyme to dry Ingredients

For fast window cleanup.

Wash with a cloth soaked in White Vinegar.

Pork Chili Verde

3 lbs. Boneless Lean Pork
Vegetable Oil
1 large Onion
3 tsp. Garlic (chopped)
1 tbsp. Cumin
4 Chili Peppers
2 Jalapenos (seeds removed) (optional)
1 Yellow Bell Pepper
2 quarts Chicken Stock
2 lbs. Tomatillos (husks removed)
1 bunch Cilantro
Salt
Pepper

Cover the bottom of a 12 inch Dutch Oven with 1/8 inch vegetable oil and heat to medium. Cut pork into desired size (1 inch squares work well). Seer pork until browned. Pour off any excess oil or fat. Puree garlic, peppers, cilantro, and tomatillos in blender until mixture is smooth. Add mixture to Dutch Oven. Add chicken stock. Bring to a slow boil. Reduce heat and simmer for 2 hours. Serve with cheese over rice and tortillas.

Quick and Easy Chili and Cornbread

3 cups cooked Pinto or Red Beans
1 1/2 lbs. Lean Hamburger
1 large jar of Garlic and Herb Sauce
1 Onion (chopped)
1/2 tsp. Garlic Powder
3 tbsp. Chili Powder
1 tsp. Thyme
1/2 tsp. Salt
1/4 tsp. Pepper

Sauté Hamburger with onions and add all remaining ingredients. Simmer for 10 to 15 minutes while you mix up your Corn Bread. Spread the corn bread mixture over the top of the chili. Replace the lid and bake on 10 to 12 briquettes in your Volcano or a very low heat on a Camp Chef propane stove. In your oven, bake at 325. If you wait for the smell you will know when it is done.

MUFFINS
BISQUITS
ROLLS
SOURDOUGH

BREADS

SOMEONE ONCE SAID THAT MAN COULD LIVE
BY EATING BREAD ALONE?
BUT OUR MOM SAID THAT GALS SHOULD HAVE
SOME RECIPES OF THEIR OWN.

Yeast Bread

Self Rising Bread

Sourdough Bread

The art of bread making has changed drastically over the years. It is not the same as when our ancestors first started baking. Our light spongy loaf of today, does not compare with the coarse ground meal, mixed with water and baked in ashes of yesterday. We will try to give you a big variety of recipes using all the basic ingredients to make your baking a simple pleasure with lots of good eating. If you should decide to try some of these recipes, remember to use the wheat sparingly unless your system is used to wheat.

To prevent splashing when frying, sprinkle a little salt in the fat before heating.

Squaw Bread

People love this one !!

4 cups Flour
1 tsp. Salt
2 tsp. Baking Powder
2 tbsp. Cornmeal
2 cups Water

Add water, slowly to the dry ingredients, mixing to a stiff dough. Knead in bowl. Pull off small pieces and shape into flat pancake. Cook in a small amount of hot fat in a heavy pan. Fat must be hot enough to bubble around the dough. Cook until brown but not crisp. Serve warm.

An apple cut in half + placed in your storage with a cake will help keep the cake fresher longer.

Western Poor Man's Bread

1 pt. Buttermilk or Sour Milk
1 tsp. Soda
A large pinch of Salt
Flour, enough to make stiff dough

Mix all ingredients together. Handle as little as possible, divide into 3 parts. Roll out or squash with your hands to about 1 inch thick. Arrange together in a pan that has been greased. Should make about 3 loaves about the size of a small pie. Bake 30 minutes in hot oven. 400 to 425 degrees. Break open like biscuit and eat warm.

Too Much Salt

In general, addition of lemon, vinegar, or brown sugar will reduce saltiness.
  Specificly:
- Beans - add brown sugar or vinegar
- Gravy - add a pinch of brown sugar
- Soup - if its the right kind, add tomatoes or sliced potatoes that stay in the soup until cooked and are then removed.

Hobo Bread in Loafs

2 cups Boiling Water
4 tsp. Soda
1 1/2 cups Raisins
4 cups Flour
1 3/4 cups Sugar
3/4 tsp. Salt
4 tbsp. Lard (or substitute)

Mix soda with raisins, and pour the boiling water over the top. Let stand overnight, covered. Add flour, salt, sugar and lard. Bake at moderate temperature (300°) for 1 hour. Put in well greased pans. Small loaf pans are best.

To sour milk, add 1 tbsp. Vinegar or Lemon Juice to sweeten Milk. Let stand for at least 5 minutes to complete action.

Injun Fry Bread

3 cups Flour
4 tsp. Baking Powder
3 tsp. Salt
2 tbsp. Sugar
1 1/4 cups lukewarm Water

Mix all ingredients together. Add the liquid all at once and mix to a biscuit dough stage. The less you handle or mix, the better. Separate them into 4 sections. Let stand for 5 minutes. Roll out to 1/8 inch thick. Fry in hot fat until golden brown. Will taste and resemble our scones of today.

Basic Dutch Oven Bread

3 cups Flour
1 tbsp. Baking Powder
1 tsp. Salt
Water to make dough

Mix dry ingredients with 3 tbsp. water to start. Add more if necessary. Work as little as possible and bake in a pre-greased Dutch Oven for 20 to 25 minutes. It can be baked as one large loaf or separated as several small. Should serve about 8 people.

VARIATIONS;
- Milk instead of Water
- 1 to 2 tbsp. Sugar
- 1 Egg
- 1 to 2 tbsp. Oil or Grease
- 1 tbsp. Cinnamon or Nutmeg

Add 1 tbsp. Vinegar to bread mixture to prevent molding.

You can still sift the one we done or come for more

Curly-Q-Pretzels

1/2 cup warm Water
1 tbsp. Yeast
1 Egg
1 tsp. Salt
1/4 cup Honey
1/4 cup Lard (or Substitute)
1 cup Milk (room temperature)
5 cups Flour

Dissolve yeast in water, mix Egg Yolk, Honey, Salt, Lard and Milk. Add to yeast mixture. Add flour a little at a time and mix well. This should make a stiff dough. If too much moisture, add more flour a little at a time. Knead well and let rise for one hour. Roll out on floured table and cut in thin strips. Twist strips and shape them any way you want. Place on greased cookie sheets and brush top with mixture of 1 tbsp. water and 1 egg. This will make twists brown. Sprinkle with salt & bake at 400 degrees, check often. Remove when brown. This is a great treat for kids.

Farmers Bread

6 Potatoes (boiled and mashed)
2 tbsp. White Sugar
2 tbsp. Butter
1 qt. lukewarm Water
6 tbsp. Yeast
2 to 3 cups flour (next morning for flour)

Mix first 4 ingredients together, into this, stir 3 cups of flour and beat to a smooth batter. Add 6 tbsp. yeast and set overnight. In the morning, knead in enough flour to make a stiff dough. Knead vigorously for 15 minutes. Set aside to rise. When double in size, knead again. Mold into loaves. Bake at 350 degrees after they have doubled in size again. This should take about 25 to 35 minutes. Put a can of water in the oven with the loaves to keep the crust soft. Brush with shortening to help brown.

Old Fashion Potato Bread

1 cup Scalded Milk
1 1/4 cups Mashed Potatoes
1/2 cup Lard (or substitute) oil shortening
1 cake Yeast
1/4 cup Sugar
2 tsp. Salt
5 or 6 cups Flour
2 Eggs

Dissolve yeast in 1/2 cup warm water & 1 tsp. Sugar, set aside. To the scalded Milk, add the Mashed Potatoes and shortening. Beat the Eggs and add to potato mixture. Add Sugar and mix well. Now add the Yeast mixture and enough flour to make a soft dough. Refrigerate and use as needed, or bake now at 300 degrees until golden brown. Brush with oil to create crisp crust.

Yam Biscuits

1 cup Mashed Yams (cooked)
1/3 cup Lard, Butter or Shortening
1 Egg
1 cup Flour
2 tsp. Baking Powder
1/2 tsp. Salt
2 tbsp. Sugar

Mix Egg, Shortening, and Yams in a bowl until fluffy. Gradually stir in the Sugar. Now add Flour, Salt and Baking Powder. Blend well and drop by tbsp. on lightly greased pan. Bake at 350 degrees until done. (15 to 20 min.) Check after 5 minutes for doneness.

Freshen hardened rolls, by sprinkling them
with a little water, put in paper bag, place
in warm oven for 10 or 15 minutes.

Country Quick Rolls or Bread

2 cups Scalded Milk
1 1/2 tsp. Salt
2 tbsp. Sugar
4 tbsp. Lard (or substitute)
4 cakes Compressed Yeast (broken)
6 cups Flour

Place hot Milk and Sugar in a bowl and stir until dissolved. When cool, add Yeast cakes broken in pieces. Stir in 1/2 Salt and 1/2 Flour. Beat well and set aside to rise until double in size. Add remaining Salt and Flour. Knead into roll or bread size balls. Place in greased pans. Allow to rise double. Brush top with melted butter, and bake at 350 degrees for 35 or 40 minutes. Will be golden brown on top. Brush again with butter. For rolls 15 to 20 minutes.

Save wrappers off of cubes of Butter or Margarine to brush across bread.

Oatmeal Trail Muffins

1 cup Oatmeal (cooked)
3 cups Flour
1 1/2 cups Milk
2 heaping tsp. Baking Powder
1/4 cup Sugar
1 Egg (well beaten)
1 tsp. Salt
1 tbsp. Butter or shortening or oil

Mix Milk in with Oatmeal at room temperature. Add all dry ingredients to Oatmeal. Now add Egg and Butter. Mix well and bake in muffin tins or Dutch Oven as bread. 25 minutes in a moderate oven.

If popcorn doesn't pop, soak in water for a few minutes. Let dry and try again.

Buttermilk Irish Soda Bread

1 1/2 cups Buttermilk (fresh if possible)
3 cups Flour
1/2 cup Sugar
1 tbsp. Baking Powder
1/2 tsp. Soda
1/2 tsp. Salt
1 1/2 cups Currents or Raisins

Mix all ingredients, except Buttermilk, together in a bowl. Add Buttermilk and stir until liquid is absorbed. Dump out on floured board and knead until dough becomes consistent. Add more Flour if sticky. Place on greased sheet and cut across in the top of dough. Bake at 350 degrees for 40 to 45 minutes. Brush top with milk or beaten egg for glaze.

A heavy cake means too much sugar or baked too short a time.

Pumpkin Day Bread
(night too)

3 1/3 cups Flour
2 tsp. Soda
1 1/2 tsp. Cinnamon
1 tsp. Nutmeg
2 1/2 cups Sugar
1 cup Shortening (melted)
4 Eggs
2/3 cups Water
2 cups Pumpkin, Squash, Carrots or Sweet Potatoes

Mix all liquid ingredients together and then add dry ingredients one at a time, mixing well after each. Put in loaf pan and bake 1 hour at 350 degrees. Great hot with whipped cream on it.

Cracks and uneven surface can be caused by too much flour, too hot an oven and by not preheating oven.

Make this one after Summer

Soda Crackers

2 cups Flour
1 tsp. Salt
1/2 tsp. Baking Soda
1/4 cup Butter (or substitute)
1/2 cup Buttermilk (or Sour Milk)
1 Egg

Put dry ingredients in bowl. Mix together and cut in the margarine. Add Buttermilk and Egg already beaten together. Mix in enough Flour to make a stiff dough. Knead thoroughly. Roll dough very thin and cut into squares of desired size. Cut round if you want. Be creative. Place on lightly greased sheet, poke with fork. Lightly sprinkle with salt. Bake at 400 degrees for 12 minutes.

Try this one with your kids :-)

VARIATION;
• Add baking powder instead of soda and sweet milk instead of sour.

Ranchhand Supreme Rolls

2 cups Flour
1/2 tsp. Salt
2 tbsp. Baking Powder
1 tsp. Cream of Tartar
3 tsp. Sugar
1/2 cup Butter
1 cup Buttermilk

Mix all dry ingredients together and add shortening. Cut in the coarse crumb consistency. Add milk all at once. Stir with fork until dough is all moist & follows fork. Pat or roll out and shape as desired. Bake on greased sheet at 400 degrees for 12 to 15 minutes. Fast and excellent in taste.

Stale bread and rolls can be crumbled and dried for use on casseroles, in puddings, dipped in egg and cinnamon and scrambled as French Toast.

Log Cabin Baking Mix

9 cups Flour
1/3 cup Baking Powder
1 1/4 cups Powdered Milk
1 1/2 cups Lard (or substitute)
4 tsp. Salt
2 tsp. Sugar

Mix all above ingredients together and cut the shortening in until it becomes a coarse meal texture. This is an all-purpose mix that can be used as Bisquick is. Add Eggs, and liquid. This can be biscuits, pancakes, etc. Store covered, in dry place and this will last for a long time. 13 cups.

Camp Biscuits

2 fistfuls Flour
2-1 finger gobs Fat
2-3 finger pinches Baking Powder
2-2 finger pinches Salt
Water (enough to moisten)

Shape dough to biscuits. Cover and cook in Dutch Oven, covered fry pan or twist and cook on stick over fire.

Basic Egg Noodles

2 Eggs
1/2 tsp. Salt
1/2 egg shell full of Cream
Flour (enough to make stiff dough)

Beat first 3 ingredients together until well mixed. Add enough Flour to make a stiff dough. Roll thin on a floured board on table. Let dry for 2 hours, and then slice to the width you desire. Should be about 1/4 inch thick, or less. Toss with remaining flour on board and cook in already prepared broth that is boiling. Cook until tender. (15 minutes)

Finger Cooking Measurements

1 finger gob	1/2 tsp.
2 finger pinch	1/8 tsp.
3 finger pinch	1/2 tsp.
4 finger pinch	1 tsp.
1 fistful	1/4 cup.

Find out how they fit your hand by measuring at home with your teaspoon and cups.

Chuckwagon Biscuits

1 cup Sourdough Starter
2 cups Flour
1/3 cup Milk
1/2 cup Butter (or melted Shortening)
2 tsp. Baking Powder
1 tsp. Salt

Mix all ingredients and pat out on floured board. Cut out, pinch off or make any shape biscuits that you want. Cook until golden brown in a Dutch Oven or regular oven at moderate temperature until golden brown. (350 degrees for 15 minutes). 25 biscuits. You'll smell them when their done. No heat in center of Dutch Oven.

The Real Meadow Muffins

1 cup Sourdough Starter
2 cups Flour
1/2 cup Milk
3/4 cups Sugar
1 Egg
2 tbsp. Lard (or substitute)
1 tsp. Baking Powder
1/2 tsp. Salt

Mix all ingredients and drop into greased muffin tins. Bake at 350 degrees for about 30 minutes. Can also be baked in small loaf pans or Dutch Oven.

VARIATIONS;

- Add berries, any kind.
- Lemon, Vanilla or Maple flavoring.
- Nuts or Raisins.

Remove odors from fat you want to reuse,
by frying potato slices in it until golden brown.
This will take out all but fish.

Sourdough - Starters - Replenish

Sourdough Starter without Yeast

2 cups Flour
1/2 tsp. Salt
2 tbsp. Sugar
2 cups warm Water

— this is the "stuff" Real

Mix all ingredients together and set aside in covered dish for 5 or 6 days. Keep in a warm place. Starter action may be delayed if too cool. Crocks are a good place to store sourdough. Always try to replenish the starter when you get down to 1 cup.

Replenisher

1 cup Flour and 1 cup Water or Milk
Sugar (if desired)

If the mixture seems to sour, just add a little Baking Soda.

Starter with Yeast

1 1/2 cups warm Water
2 cups Flour
1 tbsp. Sugar
1 tsp. Salt
1 cake Yeast

Put Yeast in warm water (not hot or it will kill yeast action), dissolve and mix in dry ingredients. Store in a covered jar or crock pot in a warm place for 1 or 2 days. Should be working and ready for any recipe.

Cowboys really carried six guns to keep robbers and thieves from stealing their sourdough starter. It's hard to eat beans without sourdough bread.

Sourdough Scratch Start

Put a cup of milk (Whole Milk) on the counter over night and be sure to cover with a light cloth. True sourdough starter will not have any commercial yeast in it. Stir in 1 cup Flour and cover again. Let the mix set a few hours and you will see the spores begin to form. Spores formed by yeast are like bees at a honey hive. If you wait long enough they will show up. Do not use a metal container or metal spoon to stir. Keep in a warm place for a few days, after this you can store in a cool place, but be sure to cover tightly. Allow mixture to warm to room temperature before using.

Just like the Chuck wagon Cooks did it.."

Sergeant Bobs Pancakes

3/4 cups Starter
1 1/2 cups Flour
1/2 cup Milk
A pinch of Salt (large)

Mix all this together and let sit over night. Should be spongy by morning.

There's a story with this one //

Add:
2 Eggs
3 tbsp. Bacon Grease
1 tsp. Soda mixed with 1 tbsp. Water
1/2 cup Sugar

Mix well to a smooth batter. If too thin, add a little more starter. Never add flour to thicken. Cook on hot griddle. Serve with maple syrup or jam.

If jelly doesn't set up when canning, use it as pancake syrup.

Mountain Muffins

1 3/4 cups Flour
3 tbsp. Sugar
1 tsp. Baking Powder
3/4 tsp. Salt
3/4 cups Milk (or Buttermilk)
6 tbsp. Lard or Shortening
2 Eggs (beaten)

Put dry ingredients in mixing bowl. Stir to combine, and add Milk, Egg and Oil. Mix well, and bake in muffin pans or drop by teaspoon in Dutch Oven and bake for 20 to 25 minutes at 375 degrees.

VARIATIONS;
- Add Cinnamon and Nutmeg to batter Add Vanilla, Almond or Lemon Flavoring
- Add Dried Fruits or Nuts
- Add Fresh Fruit or Raisins (except Pineapple fresh)
- Any Berries
- Drop 1 tsp. Jam in center before baking
- Add Chocolate Chips

Winter Snow Hotcakes

more like flapjacks

6 tbsp. Flour
1 cup Buttermilk
A pinch of Salt
6 tbsp. Fresh Snow

Stir flour, salt and snow together. Add (1 cup) Buttermilk. Bake in small cakes on hot grill, using only a very little butter. They may be eaten with butter and sugar on top. They are a very delicate cake.

Crackers for Snacks

11 cups Flour
1 tsp. Soda
1 cup Lard (or Butter)
2 tsp. Salt

Mix all ingredients thoroughly. Add cold water, enough to make stiff dough. Beat or pound with rolling pin for 15 to 20 minutes. Roll very thin and cut in squares. Sprinkle with salt. Prick with a fork and bake in a moderate temperature oven (375°) until brown. Watch carefully or they will burn.

Cow Country Buttermilk Pancakes

4 cups Flour
4 tsp. Baking Powder
4 tsp. Soda
1 1/2 tsp. Salt
4 tbsp. melted Shortening (oil)
4 Eggs
4 cups Buttermilk

Mix all ingredients together well. Cook on inverted Dutch Oven lid that has been oiled, or on heavy hot grill. This will make about 50 cakes. Serve with butter and warm maple syrup.

Here's the difference in pancakes & Flapjacks

If you get too much milk in the biscuit mix,
Drop by tsp. on greased baking sheet,
This will bake them like drop cookies.

Maple Syrup

Get 7 clean cobs that the corn has been taken off, and put in pan to boil with 3 pints of water. Boil for 1/2 hour and remove cobs. Strain if desired, and add 1 1/2 cups white sugar and 1 1/3 cups brown sugar (about 1 lb.). 2 or 3 drops of maple flavoring can be added if desired.

A handful of hickory nut shells, will also add maple flavor. Be sure to spoon out shells, they are hard on the teeth.

Sprinkle soda on oven spills. It will stop the burning odor and clean easily.

Spoon Bread

2 cups Milk
1/4 cup Butter
2 tsp. Sugar
1 tsp. Salt
2 1/2 tsp. Baking Powder
1 cup Cornmeal
2 Eggs

Boil milk in pan, add Cornmeal slowly, add Salt and stir constantly as it cooks to a soft mush. Cool and add Egg Yolks of Eggs, and Butter. Stir in Baking Powder and fold in beaten egg whites. Bake in greased baking pan for 30 minutes at 325 degrees. Serve warm. Excellent with soups and stews.

you can smell it when it's done —

The hotter you bake the less moisture in your bread. Don't over bake your bread.

Round-up Muffins

1 cup Lard (or substitute)
2 cups Sugar
4 Eggs
1 tbsp. Salt
2 cups Water
5 tsp. Soda
1 qt. Buttermilk
5 cups All Bran
5 cups Flour
(bran flakes can be substituted for all bran)

Cream Lard or substitute, with Sugar. Add Eggs one at a time. Pour in Soda, Buttermilk and Salt. Boil water and pour in at alternate time with flour mix. Let cool and stand until ready to use. This mixture will keep very well. Spoon into greased tins or in Dutch Oven. Bake at 350 degrees for 20 or 25 minutes.

Yeast breads rise faster at higher altitudes.
Be sure to keep in draft free warm place to rise.
Use a slightly warmed DO with the lid on.

Break-apart Cornbread

1/4 cup Butter (1/2 cup)
5 cups hot Water
2 cups Cornmeal
Salt to taste

Grease large jelly roll pan. Mix all ingredients together and pour into pan. Bake at 350 degrees for 25 to 35 minutes. Watch carefully. Comes from pan flat and cracked. Break into pieces and eat with soups, stews, etc.

Simple Bread. good taste.

1 tsp salt & it will make it fluffier

USE your D.O. in your Kitchen OVEN-

To keep peanut butter from sticking to the roof of your mouth, turn the sandwich upside-down.

Granny Carlsons Johnny Cakes

Put a quart of Cornmeal into the mixing bowl. Pour in a pint of warm water. Mix well and add a teaspoon of Salt. Beat well. Be sure that batter is light and fluffy. Spread batter on buttered pan, and bake well in moderate oven (325 degrees) for 30 to 40 minutes. Check often for golden brown top after 25 minutes. Cut into squares and eat warm with butter. A good variation would be to add 3 Eggs, 1 tsp. Soda and 1 qt. of Milk in place of water. 3/4 cup of Wheat Flour. This should be a batter like pancakes. Bake as above, or fry as pancakes.

The real Southern Mississip' Bread.

To soften marshmallows, place a slice of fresh bread or an apple cut in half in the sack and seal tight.

Cornbuck Bread

2 cups Cornmeal
1 tsp. Salt
3 tbsp. Butter
1 1/2 cups boiling Water
2 tbsp. Bacon Grease (or Lard)

Put 1 1/2 cups water in a pan and bring to a boil. Mix dry ingredients and pour in boiling water. Stir to a thick dough. Wet hands and form into pone patties, about biscuit size. Fry in grease until golden brown. Remove and drain. Serve with Cactus Jelly. Using a small Dutch Oven, can prove to be helpful with hot fat. Remember to put a few grains of salt into the greased pan to help keep the splatter down. Bake for 25 to 35 minutes in either oven at 325 degrees.

Baked in a Dutch Oven are small is gre---at.

Southwest Corn Bread

Something brown

2 cups Cornmeal
2 1/2 tsp. Baking Powder
1 tsp. Salt
3 tbsp. Flour
2 cups Milk
3 Eggs
2 tbsp. Bacon Grease (or Lard)

1/2 C chopped Bacon, it was great taste

Mix dry ingredients together and then pour in the Milk. Add Eggs 1 at a time, mixing well after each. Pour in cooled, melted grease. Pour mixture into Dutch Oven that has been lightly greased. Or, into a long pan that has been greased. Bake 30 to 40 minutes in either oven at 320 degrees.

VARIATIONS;
• Add pimentos, green peppers or corn.
• Add jalapeños too.

Anything cooked in a Dutch Oven can be converted to a regular stove oven, and vice-versa.

Pilgrim's Bread
(John Wayne Style)

4 1/2 cups White Flour
1/2 cup Rye Flour
1/2 cup Whole Wheat Flour
3/4 cups Cornmeal
1/3 cup Brown Sugar
1 1/2 tbsp. Salt
1/4 cup melted Shortening (or lard)
1/2 cup warm Water
2 Yeast Cakes
2 cups boiling Water

Combine together in bowl, Cornmeal, Brown Sugar and Salt. Stir in 2 cups boiling water. Add Shortening and allow to cool. Put yeast in 1/2 cup warm water and dissolve. Add to mixture. Now beat in remaining ingredients. Knead well until dough is smooth. Grease well and put in bowl to rise double in size. Punch down and divide dough. Bake 40 to 45 minutes in 325 degree oven.

Add a few teaspoons of sugar and a sprinkle of cinnamon to some water and bring to a boil in a pan.
It will make your kitchen smell like you have cooked all day. A slice of onion works too.

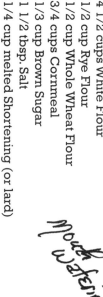

Indian Zuni Bread

1/4 cup Water (room temp)
1/2 cup Butter
1 Yeast Cake
2 cups Cornmeal
2 tsp. Salt
1/2 cup Molasses
2 cups Flour
1 3/4 cups boiling Water

Ahead of time, dissolve yeast in 1/4 cup of water. Mix Cornmeal, Salt, Butter and Molasses in a bowl. Pour boiling water over mixture and add Flour and Yeast after mixture cools down. Beat about 100 strokes. If not a soft dough, add a small amount of flour. Wait 10 minutes and knead 100 times. Let rise until double. Punch down, divide in two and place on greased cookie sheet. With a nail or a pointed knife, put 5 or 6 holes in top of round loaf. Let rise until puffed. Bake at 325 degrees for 25 or 30 minutes.

Fall and Winter Squash Bread

3 Eggs
1 cup melted Shortening
2 cups Sugar
3 tsp. Vanilla
2 1/2 cups Grated, Peeled Squash
3 cups Flour
1 tsp. Salt
1 tsp. Soda
3 tsp. Cinnamon
1 tsp. Nutmeg
1/4 tsp. Baking Powder
1 cup Nuts

Mix well the Eggs, Sugar, Vanilla, Shortening and Squash. Sift in dry ingredients and mix well after each. Stir in Nuts. Bake in 2 loaf pans, at moderate heat (350 degrees) for 1 hour.

Rocky Edge Popovers

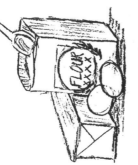

2 cups Flour
3 Eggs
2 cups Milk
1/2 tsp. Salt
2 tbsp. Melted Butter

Mix Eggs and Milk together in a bowl. Add dry ingredients and beat until bubbles form on top of batter. Pour into hot greased muffin pans. Bake at hot temperature (400 degrees) for 35 to 40 minutes. Decrease heat and serve within 5 minutes. Usually hollow inside.

If bread does not rise, it can be caused from old yeast, over kneading or water is too hot when dissolving.

Fresh Apple Bread

1 cup Sugar
1 cup Lard
2 Eggs
1 1/4 cups Finely Chopped Apples
2 cups Flour
2 tbsp. Buttermilk
1/2 tsp. Salt
1 tsp. Soda
1 tsp. Vanilla
1 cup Nuts (Pecans)

Mix all ingredients together and pour in a greased loaf pan. Sprinkle the top of the bread with cinnamon and sugar. Bake at 300 degrees for 1 hour or until you can smell it. 10 inch Dutch Oven works great.

Enough to make you happy all over...

Nut Graham Bread

2 cups Graham Flour (Wheat Flour)
2 cups White Flour
2 tsp. Salt
2 tbsp. Baking Powder
1 1/2 cups Sugar
2 Eggs (beaten)
2 cups Milk
1 cup Walnuts

Mix Eggs together with the Sugar in a large bowl. Add all the dry ingredients and beat well with the Milk. Pour into greased pans. Let stand for 25 minutes and bake in moderate oven at 325 degrees for 1 hour. Makes 2 loaves. Bakes well in Cast Iron Bread Pans at 300 degrees.

When frying donuts, put a few drops of vinegar in the oil before heating and it will keep the donuts from getting grease soaked.

Danish Ebleskewers

2 cups Buttermilk
2 cups Flour
3 Eggs
1 tsp. Baking Powder
1/2 tsp. Salt
1 tsp. Soda
2 tsp. Sugar
2 finger pinch of Nutmeg

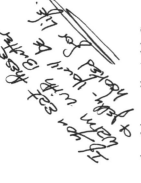

Put Egg Yolks in bowl and whip well. Add Sugar, Salt and Milk. Mix well, add Soda, Flour and Baking Powder. Fold in Egg Whites. Heat cast iron pan to hot stage and drop by spoonfuls in greased section. Turn with fork to cook on both sides. Add 1 can of Apple Pie Filling to batter for a great variation, or drop 1/2 tsp. of Jam in the batter before you turn them.

Simple Fritters

1 1/3 cups Flour
1/4 tsp. Salt
2 tsp. Baking Powder
2 tbsp. Sugar
1 Egg
2/3 cups Buttermilk

Sift together dry ingredients. Add Egg and Milk. Mix well, batter should be just thick enough to coat vegetables or fruit or meats. If too thin, add flour.

VARIATIONS;

• Can of whole kernel corn.
• Blueberries (any berry).
• Any fresh vegetable, dip and deep fry.
• Small pieces of chopped cooked meat.

To make quick bread crumbs, freeze fresh bread and grate it.

Danish Stollen Bread

2 cakes or pkgs. Yeast
1/2 cup lukewarm Water
5 cups Flour
3/4 cups Sugar (prefer powdered)
2 tbsp. Lemon Juice or orange flavoring
1 1/4 tsp. Salt
1/2 tsp. Cinnamon
Large pinch Mace
1 cup Milk (scalded)
2 Eggs (well beaten)
1/2 cup Butter (melted)
1/2 cup Currants
1/2 cup Raisins
1/2 cup Candied Fruit (if available)

from the old Country A Thanksgiving & Christmas treat.

Soften yeast in lukewarm water and let stand for 10 minutes. Place powdered sugar in bowl with salt and spices. Add hot milk and stir until sugar dissolves. Cool to lukewarm so you won't kill the yeast action. Beat in 1 cup flour and then the eggs. Be sure to mix well after each addition. Add 1 more cup of flour and mix well. Gradually beat in yeast mixture and beat until smooth.

Add cooled Butter, 2 more cups of Flour, lemon juice and beat with wooden spoon until the mixture is smooth. Mix all fruits and berries together and sprinkle with 1 cup flour. Mix thoroughly into dough. Remove from bowl to floured cloth or board. Let sit for 10 minutes. Knead for 10 minutes or until smooth and elastic. Add about 1/4 cup more flour if needed. Now shape into ball. Place in clean, well greased bowl and grease top with melted butter. Cover and let rise in warm place. Knead on floured board, and shape into a ball. Let rest 10 minutes. Place rolling pin in center and roll out both ways to shape as omelet. Brush on Egg mixture. Let rise, when double, bake in 350 degree oven for 45 minutes. Ice while hot. **Terrific.**

TOPPING:

1 Egg
1 tbsp. Milk (mix well)

ICING:

1/4 tsp. Vanilla
1 cup Powdered Sugar
3 tsp. Milk
1 tsp. White Corn Syrup

On the Trail Donuts

3 cups Flour
1 cup Sugar
1/2 tsp. Salt
1 tsp. Baking Powder
1 tsp. Butter
1/2 tsp. Cinnamon
1/2 tsp. Nutmeg
3/4 cups Milk
2 Eggs
Shortening (melted)

Mix together all the dry ingredients; slowly add the Milk while stirring. Add 2 Eggs to the batter and stir well. On a floured surface (the tailgate of the wagon) roll or pat out to a thickness of 1/2 inch or less. Cut into squares and poke your finger thru the middle. Drop into hot oil. When brown on one side, turn and cook on opposite side. Remove and let drain on towel. Place in bag with Sugar and Cinnamon. Shake and eat. Makes 50 medium size or enough for the trail crew.

Barnfields Cowboy talk... good.

Carrot Bread

Cream together:
1 cup Sugar
2 Eggs
1/2 cup Lard (or substitute)

Add and mix well:
1 1/2 cups Flour
1/2 tsp. Salt
1 tsp. Soda
1 tsp. Cinnamon

Add:
1 1/2 cups grated raw Carrots
1/2 cup Nuts
1/2 tsp. Nutmeg

Mix well, bake in large loaf pan at 300 degrees for 1 hour. Check for doneness by inserting a toothpick.

Bread crust that's dark and blisters is caused by under rising & cooking at high temp.

Cattails – Our Free Food - Available

One of the most common weeds we have is *Cattails*.

They are found almost everywhere in this country. They are very easy to prepare, quite tasty, and nutritious. They can be used more months of the year than any other food. You will find them in most wet places and along streams. In spring time you can gather the sprouts, husk off the paper like shell in which they grow, steam for a few minutes and eat hot. They make an excellent vegetable.

These sprouts can be enjoyed all summer, because Cattails have a long blooming season. The flower appears, and boiled and eaten just like corn. When the bloom appears and goes to a soft pollen, they can be rubbed, scraped into a bowl and eaten. Pound for pound, this is richer in protein than meat. Pounded out, it becomes powdery and can be substituted for 1/2 the flour in any recipe.

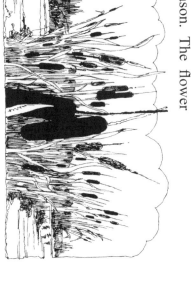

The Indians used the roots for flour. They dig, wash and peel the roots, then crushed them with their hands and put them into a pail of water. The flour would settle to the bottom and as it did, the root particles were washed away. Then they would dry the flour and crush it in their matates with a manos. They would combine it with cornmeal and any other flour that they made. It's no wonder the Shoshoni and Utes lived so well before the White Man. The flour is rich in protein. Give it a try sometime, just for the pleasant experience of eating.

I try this on often in my scouts pancakes & Breads

Cattail Flapjacks
Old Shorty's

2 cups Cattail Pollen (Flowers)
2 cups Wheat Flour
4 tsp. Baking Powder
2 Eggs
1/2 cup Evaporated Milk (or Cream)
1 1/2 cups Water
2 tbsp. Bacon Drippings (Grease)

Beat the eggs, add Milk, Water, Bacon Grease and mix well. Add all the dry ingredients and stir until the mixture is smooth and creamy. Fry in hot grease until brown.

Cattails

- The flower spikes can be husked out of their sheaths.

- Put them into boiling water and cook until tender.

- After the plant has matured, the roots may be gathered.

The roots will have the best food value in the fall. The inner root will have a sweet, starchy taste. They can be eaten raw or cooked in the same way you would potatoes. They will be a bit stringy, but can also be dried and ground to a meal and used like flour.

Happiness Cake
(This recipe is for our friends.)

1 cup Consideration for Others
2 cup Sacrifice
3 cup Forgiveness
2 cup Kind Deeds
1 cup Good Thoughts
1 cup Service to Others

Mix thoroughly with love and kindness; add tears of joy and happiness. Fold in 4 cups of your prayers and faith. Flavor with visiting the elderly and friends. Bake well with smiles that are given every day. This could be served daily with a hug.

A message to family + friends

Leftover Ham Canapes

Toast slice bread and lightly butter. Cut slices of bread and ham in 4 quarters. Lightly spread mustard on each piece. Sprinkle with grated cheese of your choice, cheddar, monterey jack, swiss or a combination. Melt cheese under the broiler or warm in oven of 375 enough to melt cheese.

The Farmer's Almanac is a popular book, just because of the helpful hints to others and the things it shares with the world. Try sharing your talents and see how popular you get.

Bread Leftovers

My mom always kept a large can container in the pantry for dry bread. After she baked bread, everything that got too done or was left open on the cupboard was put in the can to complete the drying process. Then the most wonderful puddings, cakes, dressing, cookies and etc. was made. Mom would save white bread, French bread, rolls of any kind & wheat bread in the same can. Leftover corn bread was saved also for great muffins and waffles. Whenever Mom needed crumbs, out would come the rolling ping or the food grinder and it was a fun thing to make bread crumbs. Mom kept the crumbs in a separate container and made sure there was always plenty around. The crumbs were great on top of vegetable dishes and when she would chicken fry squash or meat it was wonderful.

One fun thing I remember most, is when she would cut the crust from the bread and fry it in butter in a skillet on the coal stove. When it was brown on one side, she would make a hole in the center, turn it over, and put an egg in the hole.

This was so fun to eat and she'd always make it decorative and taste wonderful. Sometimes she'd take chunks of dried bread, dip it in a beaten egg and fry it in a bacon greased skillet. When it was done, she'd sprinkle it with cinnamon and sugar and serve those chunks with maple syrup she made herself. We put buttered toasted bread crumbs on dandelion greens in the spring and summer with moms homemade dressings and it was great.

If we had leftover muffins, mom would scrape out the center, put some homemade butter in and reheat in the oven. Then she would fill them with homemade jelly or marmalade. Believe me we didn't have a lot of money when I was young, but my mom was a great cook.

Use your imagination and let your creative cooking talents go to work for you too.

Salt Rising Potato Water Bread

1/2 cup Flour
2 tbsp. Sugar
2 pkgs. Dry Yeast
1/2 cup Sugar
1/4 cup Cooking Oil
2 tbsp. Salt
5 cups Potato Water
6 cups Flour

Combine 1/2 cup flour & 2 tbsp. sugar, with 2 packages dry yeast and 1 cup potato water. Cover, let stand 4 hours. Add remaining potato water and 1/2 cup sugar. Cover and let stand overnight. Next day stir start, remove 1 cup of liquid and add 2 tbsp. sugar. Pour into glass jar, cover and refrigerate. To remaining 4 cups, add oil, salt, and enough flour to make a moderately stiff dough. Place in a large greased bowl. Let rise in a warm place till double. Stir down. Divide dough in thirds. Place in greased pans. Let rise till double. Bake at 375 for 50 minutes.

a light bread good for sandwiches

Leftover Bread Dressing for Chicken

8 to 10 heaping cups Dry Bread
1 large Onion (chopped)
1 1/2 cups chopped Celery & Carrots
2 tbsp. Log Cabin Seasoning
1 tsp. Pepper
1 tbsp. Salt
1 tbsp. Garlic
4 tbsp. Sage
8 Eggs
3 cups Chicken Broth

use this one with all meats

Put all ingredients in a large bowl and pour chicken broth over the top. If bread is extra dry, you may need more liquid. Mix all ingredients until moist. Stuff bird or place in pan as a loaf and bake. 375 for 45 to 60 minutes.

Save Potato Water from Boiling Potatoes to Make Breads.

Quick Potato Bread

4 cups Warm Water
2 pkgs. Dry Yeast
4 tbsp. Sugar
6 tbsp. Oil
1 1/2 cups Mashed Potatoes
8 to 10 cups Flour

Measure warm water into large mixing bowl. Sprinkle yeast into water, allow to dissolve. Add sugar, oil, salt, potatoes, and 5 cups flour. Beat until smooth. Add remaining flour to make moderately stiff dough. Knead until smooth and satiny. Place in greased bowl, turn to grease the top and let rise until double in bulk. About 1 hour. Punch down, divide in 4ths. Place in pans. Bake 350 for 35 minutes. Excellent taste.

Potato Ranch Rolls

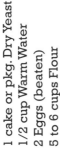

1 cup Scalded Milk
1 cup Mashed Potatoes
1/2 cup Shortening
1/4 cup Sugar
2 tsp. Salt
1 cake or pkg. Dry Yeast
1/2 cup Warm Water
2 Eggs (beaten)
5 to 6 cups Flour

Scald milk, add sugar, shortening, salt, and potatoes. Cool. Dissolve yeast in warm water, add to milk mixture. Add eggs and 1/2 flour. Beat well, cover and let rise 1 hour. Stir in remaining flour to make a stiff dough. Knead, place in greased bowl, cover and place in refrigerator overnight. Make desired rolls when ready. Parker house, ranch, spud nuts, fry bread, cinnamon rolls, etc. Bake rolls in hot (400 deg.) oven. You can smell them when they're done.

I Wish I Retained as Much Heat as My Dutch Oven.

Leftover Cornmeal Zucchini Muffins

3/4 cups Leftover Zucchini (cooked or raw)
1/2 tsp. Salt
1 1/4 cups Flour
3/4 cups Cornmeal
1 tbsp. Baking Powder
2 tsp. Sugar
3/4 tsp. Salt
2/3 cups Buttermilk or Sour Milk
3 tbsp. Oil
1 Egg
1/2 cup Grated Cheddar Cheese
1 large Green Onion (chopped)

Grate or mash zucchini, set aside. Combine flour, cornmeal, baking powder, sugar & salt. Mix together in a separate bowl, buttermilk, oil, & egg. Add zucchini to dry ingredients with cheese and green onion. Pour in buttermilk mix all at once. Mix until dry ingredients are evenly moistened. Divide into greased muffin tins. Bake 425 for 30 minutes. Loosen edges with knife when done. Two finger pinch of cayenne pepper can be added to dry ingredients, if desired.

Sour Milk Biscuits

1 cup Leftover Sour Milk or Cream
2 cups Flour
1/2 tsp. Salt
1/2 tsp. Baking Soda
1 tsp. Baking Powder
4 tbsp. Shortening

Mix and sift all dry ingredients together. Cut in shortening until texture of cornmeal. Add milk & mix. Knead lightly on floured board. Roll to 1/2 in thickness, cut with floured cutter or tuna can. Bake hot at 450 degrees for 12 to 15 minutes.

using up that sour milk or cream

Romeo was known as the First Social Climber.

Sour Milk Bran Muffins

2 Eggs
1/2 cup Sugar
1/4 cup Molasses
1 1/2 cups Leftover Sour Milk
2 1/2 tbsp. Melted Butter
1 1/2 cups Flour
1 tsp. Salt
1 1/2 tsp. Baking Soda
2 1/2 cups Bran
1/2 cup Nuts (or Raisins - optional)

Beat eggs, add sour milk, sugar, molasses and butter. In separate bowl, sift all dry ingredients together. Add raisins, nuts or other fruits then blend in the liquid only enough to moisten all dry ingredients. Fill greased muffin tins 2/3 full & bake 25 minutes at 400 degrees.

Leftover Sour Cream Biscuits

2 cups Flour
1 tsp. Baking Soda
1 tsp. Baking Powder
1 tsp. Salt
1 cup Leftover Sour Cream

Sift dry ingredients together and gradually work into the cream making a soft dough. Roll out 1/2 in. thick & cut with biscuit cutter or tuna can. Can be any shape. Place in greased 12" Dutch Oven or on a greased cookie sheet. Bake 12 to 15 minutes at 400 degrees. This recipe can be used as a pastry for meat pie, as shortcakes or for filling with meat mixture to bake.

Of Course I Don't Work as Hard as the Men in a Contest.

I use a Volcano.

Hush Puppies

1 1/2 cups Cornmeal
1/2 cup Flour
2 tsp. Baking Powder
1/2 tsp. Salt
3/4 cups Milk
1 Onion (grated)
1 Egg

Combine all dry ingredients in a bowl. In a second bowl mix the Egg, Milk and Onion. Now blend together and drop a teaspoon of mixture in a pot of hot oil or grease. When puppies are golden take from hot fat and drain on towel. Serve hot. A variation could be to add corn or some type of fruit or berry.

try this one - it's Southern

Hush Puppies came from long ago, when the hunters would tie there dogs to the tree while they cooked their meal. The cook would toss the leftovers to the dogs, calling "Hush Puppies". It was usually the bread that was leftover -- thus the way that "Hush Puppies" was named.

Ponehaws

1 1/2 lb. Pork
1/4 lb. Pork Liver (optional)
1 cup Yellow Cornmeal
2 tsp. Salt
1/2 cup Onions (chopped)
1/2 tsp. Thyme
1/2 tsp. Dried Sage
1/2 tsp. Majoram
1/2 tsp. Pepper
1/4 tsp. Garlic

In a sauce pan, put 1 quart of water and the Pork meat. Cook over a moderate heat for one hour. Drain and keep the broth for later. Clean the meat from any bones and cut in small pieces. In another saucepan, blend Cornmeal, Salt, 1 cup of broth and cook until thick. Stir constantly to keep from sticking. When mixture is thick, stir in meat, onions and all seasonings. Cover and simmer gently for 45 minutes. Be sure the heat is very low. Pour into a loaf pan and chill until firm. When ready to serve, cut into slices, dust with flour, and fry in a small amount of shortening until crisp on both sides. Serve at once.

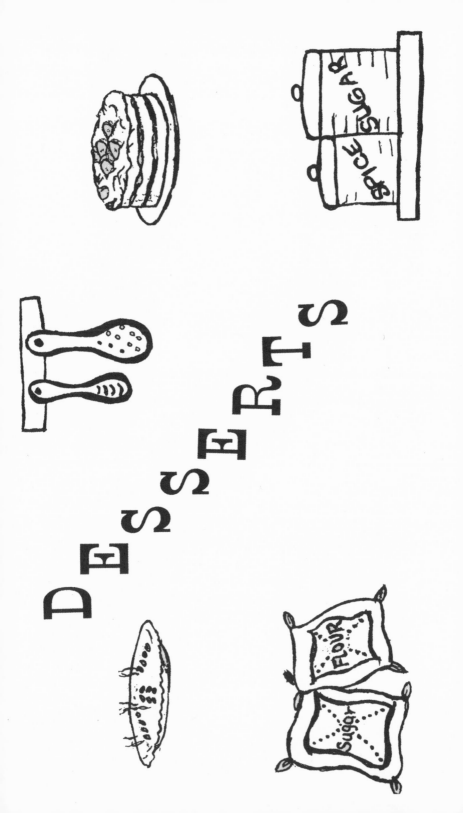

DESSERTS

Papa Niles Chocolate Sauerkraut Cake

1 1/2 cups Sugar
1/2 cup Lard (or substitute)
3 Eggs
1 tsp. Vanilla
2 cups Flour
1 tsp. Soda
1 tsp. Baking Powder
1/4 tsp. Salt
1/2 cup Cocoa
1 cup Water
1 cup Sauerkraut (rinsed, drained & finely cut)

Cream Sugar and lard until light and fluffy. Add Eggs 1 at a time and beat well after each. Add Vanilla. Add all dry ingredients, alternating with water. Beat until smooth after each addition. Stir in Sauerkraut. Pour into a greased baking dish that has been lightly floured. Bake at 350 degrees for 35 to 40 minutes. 3 loaf pans or 9x13 cake pan. Cool and frost.

Homemade Mayo Cake

2 cups Flour
2 tsp. Soda
1 cup boiling Water
1 cup Sugar
1 cup Mayonnaise
1/2 cup Cocoa
1 1/2 tsp. Vanilla

Mix one by one the ingredients in order. Grease and flour 2 loaf tins or 2 round pans. Bake cake in moderate oven (350 degrees) for 25 to 35 minutes for loaf tins, and 20 to 25 for round pans. Test cake for doneness after 20 minutes. Frost when cake is cold. Excellent for company.

Grating a stick of butter,
will soften it very quickly.

Do Without Cake

2 cups Brown Sugar
2 cups Currants (or Raisins)
2 1/2 tsp. Cinnamon
1 tsp. Cloves
1/4 tsp. Salt
1 1/2 tsp. Nutmeg
1 cup Lard (or substitute)
2 cups boiling Water
2 tsp. Soda
3 1/2 cups Flour

Add all ingredients but Soda to a pan and boil over an open fire for 2 minutes. Remove and cool. Add Soda already dissolved in a small amount of water. Then stir in 3 1/2 cups of Flour (sifted). Bake in a 9x13 pan or two layer pans. Grease and flour the bottoms. Bake at 350 degrees for 25 to 30 minutes. Check for doneness at about 20 minutes. Cake should pull from the sides of the pan when done.

Easy, fast, + good

This cake was a must in the early Pioneer days.

Hickory Nut Spice Cake

1/2 cup Lard (or substitute)
1 1/2 cups Sugar
3 large Eggs
1 tsp. Baking Powder
3 cups Flour
1 cup Buttermilk
1 cup Hickory Nuts (chopped, or substitute)
1 tsp. Cinnamon

Mix Lard and Sugar together well. Add Milk and then Egg Yolks well beaten. Add sifted Flour, Baking Powder and then the Nuts. Lastly fold in the beaten Egg Whites. Pour carefully into a pan, 9x13, and bake at 350 to 375 degrees for 25 minutes. Use standard test for doneness. Frost when cool or serve warm with whipped cream.

Autumn Squash Cake

1/2 cup Shortening
1 cup Brown Sugar
1 cup White Sugar
2 Eggs (well beaten)
1 cup cooked Squash, Pumpkin, or Carrots
3 cups Flour (sifted)
4 tsp. Baking Powder
1/4 tsp. Soda
1/2 cup Buttermilk (or Sour Milk)
1 cup Nuts
1 tsp. Maple Flavoring (or Vanilla)

(Bonnie's favorite)

Mix together till fluffy, Shortening & Sugars. Add Eggs and Squash, mixing well again. Mix all dry ingredients together and add to cream mixture, alternating with Milk. Fold Nuts and flavoring into the batter, and bake in a 350 to 375 degree oven for 30 minutes. Test for doneness by inserting a broom straw in the cake. If it comes out clean, the cake is done. Also, if the cake pulls from the sides of the pan, it will be done. Do not overcook. Dry cakes are not good. This is a large recipe and takes a 9x13 pan or makes 2 1/2 dozen cupcakes.

Apple Pie Harvest Cake

; You have to "try this one"

3 tbsp. Shortening
1 Egg
1/2 cup Nuts
1 cup Sugar
3/4 tsp. Cinnamon & Nutmeg
1/2 tsp. Salt & Baking Powder
1 tsp. Soda & Vanilla
1 1/4 cups Flour
3 cups Apples (peeled and diced)

Mix well, Shortening, Sugar and Egg. Add all remaining ingredients and mix only enough to moisten flour. Spread in Pie tin and bake for 40 to 45 minutes at 350 degrees. This is a great dessert to serve warm and with Whipped Cream or Ice Cream.

*If sugar is lumpy, sift before measuring.
Powdered sugar should be sifted if you measure
for a true measurement.*

Creek Water Cake

1/4 cup Butter (or substitute)
1 cup Sugar
2 1/2 cups Flour
1 cup cold creek Water
3 Eggs
1/2 tsp. Salt
2 1/2 tsp. Baking Powder

Stir Butter & Sugar to a fine cream. Add Egg Yolks, beat well. Add Water a little at a time alternating with the Flour, Salt and Baking Powder. Whip Egg Whites in separate pan and blend with flour mixture. Do not stir except to blend together. Bake in a moderate oven (350°) for 25 minutes. Check after 25 minutes for doneness.

Old people are the life of the party; Even if it lasts 'till 9:00 pm.

Washington's Currant Delight
(This recipe dates back to about 1760 in Missouri)

2 cups Butter (or substitute)
3 cups Sugar
4 cups Flour
2 tsp. Baking Powder
5 Eggs
1 cup Buttermilk
1/2 cup Currants (Raisins can be substituted)
1 tsp. Nutmeg
1 tsp. Cinnamon
1/4 cup Dried Fruit

Mix Butter and Sugar to a light cream. Add beaten Eggs gradually and combine with dry ingredients mixing well after each addition. Add remaining ingredients and mix to a smooth batter. Bake in a shallow long pan in a rather quick and steady heated oven (375°). Test for doneness after 45 to 50 minutes. Could take 1 1/2 hours. Frost with white icing or serve with whipped cream.

Old Farm Fruit Cake

2 cups Dried Apples (soak overnight)

Make batter of;
1 cup Butter
1 cup Sugar
3 Eggs
1 cup Sour Cream or Buttermilk
1 tsp. Soda (mix with Milk)
1 tsp. Cinnamon, Cloves & Nutmeg
5 cups Flour
1 cup Raisins or Currants

Chop apples in the morning and cook well in 2 cup molasses. Cool and roll in flour. Mix all remaining ingredients and add the apples. Bake in a moderate oven for 1 hour or whatever time it takes to be done (350º). Test for doneness after 1 hour.

On the Trail Applesauce Cake

Cream together 1/2 cup Lard or a good substitute, with 1 cup Sugar. Add 1 cup Applesauce and mix well. Add 1 3/4 cups Flour, 1 tsp. Soda, 1/2 tsp. Salt, Nutmeg and Allspice. Mix well. Add 1 cup Raisins or Currants that have been lightly floured. This recipe does not call for an egg, but if you have one throw it in. Bake in a moderate oven (350º) until done. Can be served with a cup of trail coffee or fresh cow's milk. This is also great in a Dutch Oven as a topping for cobbler.

Before measuring a sticky liquid, oil the cup or spoon with cooking oil and rinse in hot water.
This will allow all the honey or etc. to drain from the cup.

Grandma's Boiled Fruitcake

1 cup Sugar
1 cup Raisins
1 1/4 cups Water
1 tsp. Vanilla
1 cup Shortening
2 cups Flour
1/2 cup or more of Nuts
1 Egg
1 tsp. Cinnamon
1 tsp. Soda
1 tsp. Cloves
1/2 tsp. Salt

Boil 3 minutes, Cloves, Cinnamon, Water, and Raisins. Set aside to cool. Mix well, Sugar, Shortening and Egg. Add remaining ingredients and boiled mixture. Bake in moderate oven until done. About 40 to 50 minutes at 350°. Good cake for the holidays, as it stays moist if you don't overcook. Dried fruits and cherries can be added for variety.

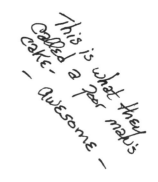

This is what they called a "poor cake". Awesome —

Fruit Cake Spiced Cookies

1 lb. Butter
6 Eggs
2 cups Sugar
2 tsp. Vanilla
7 cups Flour
1 cup Nuts
2 cups Currants or Raisins
1 1/2 lb Fruitcake Mix
2 tsp. Soda
1/2 cup Dried Cherries
4 tbsp. Brandy, Wine, or Moonshine

Boil Raisins in a small amount of water, cool and set aside the liquid in case you need it for the batter. Mix all ingredients together except the flour. Add the flour 1 cup at a time. If the dough is too stiff, add a little of the raisin water. Drop by tsp. on to a cookie sheet and bake at 275° for 20 to 25 minutes. This will make a lot of cookies so's that you can freeze some for the holidays. Be sure to cover and store, to keep them from drying out.

Toss freshly cut fruit in lemon juice to keep it from going dark. Or, cover it with simple syrup made from equal parts of sugar and water and cooked till syrupy.

Mama's Jellyroll Delight

1 cup Sugar
4 large Eggs
2 cups Flour
2 1/2 tbsp Melted Butter
1 tsp Baking Powder
1 tsp Lemon Juice
1/4 tsp Salt
4 tbsp. Milk or Cream
Jelly [Your Choice]

Cream Eggs and Sugar together, sift in Flour, Salt and Baking Powder. Melt Butter and add to mixture with juice and cream. Grease pan and dust with flour. Pour in batter and spread evenly. Bake for 12 minutes at 350° and turn out of pan onto powdered sugared paper. Spread quickly with jelly and roll up immediately. Cake will crack if it cools off. The faster you work the better. Sliced jelly roll is delicious served with a spoon of homemade pudding or Ice Cream.

Blackberry Shortcake

Bake jelly roll cake as in the recipe. Cut into 4 pieces. Take the 4 cups of blackberries that you have previously soaked in sugar water and drained over 2 of the cake squares. Spread whipped cream on them and top with the other two squares. A few berries and some whipped cream on top will add a nice taste as well as enhance the flavor. Sprinkle powdered sugar on top just before you serve.

Hardened Brown Sugar placed in a bowl with a slice of fresh bread and covered will soften in a few hours. If you need it in a hurry, simply grate the brown sugar to what you need. 30 seconds in a microwave.

Oatmeal Cake Topping

1/2 cup Butter
1/2 cup Brown Sugar
1/3 cup Evaporated Milk
1 tsp. Vanilla
3/4 cup Chopped Nuts
3/4 cup Coconut (if available)

Put all ingredients in pan over low heat. Blend well and spread over cake while warm. Also good on spice cake or devil's food cake.

Jelly Meeting Day Cake

1 qt. Flour (4 cups)
2 Eggs
Salt to taste
1 cup Heavy Cream

Mix together and work well, roll as thin as paper. Bake until brown. While warm, cover with jelly and roll up like a rug. Hold together with broom straws or toothpicks.

Brown Betty – Granny's Way

2 cups soft Bread Crumbs
2 tbsp. Butter
3 cups Apples (peeled and chopped up)
1/2 cup Sugar
1/4 tsp. Cinnamon
1/2 tsp. Nutmeg
1/4 cup Water
1/2 Lemon (juiced and grate the rind)

Mix the Apples and all ingredients except the Butter and Bread Crumbs. Grease a 9x13 pan. Put alternate layers of bread and apple mixture in pan. Melt butter and pour over the mixture. Bake at 375° until apples are done and top layer is brown. Bake the first 20 minutes covered and the last 15 or 20 minutes uncovered.

Dip a new broom in salt water to help it last and stay together longer.

Huckleberry or Elderberry Pie

3 large cups of Berries
2/3 cups Sugar
2 tbsp. Vinegar
2 or 3 tbsp. of Flour
1 9" Pie Shell (unbaked)

Put washed berries in pie crust. Combine sugar and vinegar, pour over the berries. Dust pie with flour and seal with top crust. You can substitute lemon juice for the vinegar. Bake in a hot oven (425°) for 15 minutes and then in a 350° oven for 25 minutes. Pies sometimes boil over, so be sure to place on a cookie sheet or tin foil.

Rhubarb Country Pie

2 cups Rhubarb (cut & cleaned)
1 cup Sugar
3 tbsp. Flour
1 large Egg
1/2 tsp. Cinnamon and Nutmeg

1 cup sliced strawberries great
strawberries makes

Mix sugar and flour together in same bowl. Add egg and mix well. Add the rhubarb and pour into unbaked pie shell. Sprinkle with cinnamon and nutmeg very lightly. Cover with top crust and bake at 450° for 10 minutes, and 375° for 40 minutes. 1 cup of strawberries can be added to this pie.

If cake sticks to the pan, place on cold damp rag and let stand for a few minutes.

Currant or Gooseberry Double Crust Pie

2 1/2 cups Washed Fruit
1 cup Brown Sugar
3 tbsp. Cream or Evaporated Milk
1/2 tsp. Vanilla
2 Eggs
1/4 cup Butter

Cream the Butter & Sugar. Beat the Eggs and fold in gently. Now add the Fruit, Vanilla and Milk. Mix well and pour in an unbaked pie shell. Place the top crust over the pie, seal and bake at 425° for 15 minutes. Lower the heat and bake at 350° for 20 minutes.

Granny's Gooseberry Pie

4 cups Gooseberries (washed)
2 Eggs (slightly beaten)
2 tbsp Cornstarch
1/4 cup Flour
2 cups Sugar
1/4 tsp. Salt, Nutmeg, & Cinnamon
1/8 tsp Cloves

Lightly mix Eggs with Gooseberries. Blend all dry ingredients in with the berries. Combine thoroughly and pour into pie shell. Place small amounts of butter around the pie and cover with the top crust. Seal the edges and bake in a hot oven (450°) for 10 minutes. Then bake 40 minutes more at 350°. Brushing the top of the crust with milk or egg mixture will give it a brown glaze.

Grandma's Pumpkin Pie Surprize

1 3/4 cups Pumpkin (Squash, Carrots or Yams)
1 cup Sugar
3 Eggs (beaten)
1/2 tsp Cinnamon, Nutmeg, Salt, & Ginger
1 cup Cream or Evaporated Milk

Mix well beaten Eggs with Pumpkin and Sugar. Add all spices and milk. Mix well. Pour into an unbaked pie shell, 9" or bigger. Bake at 425° for 15 minutes, then turn oven down to 375° for 30 minutes. Pie should be golden brown and firm. Great with freshly whipped cream.

Southern Raisin Pie

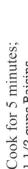

"Grandma Bailey made this with her eyes closed."

Cook for 5 minutes;
1 1/2 cups Raisins
1 1/2 cups Water
1 1/2 cups Brown Sugar
2 tbsp. Butter

Now add;
2 Beaten Egg Yolks
1 tsp. Lemon Juice
3 tbsp. Cornstarch (dissolved in)
3 tbsp. Water

Cook for 5 minutes, stirring almost constantly. Remove from fire and cool slightly. Pour into baked crust. Allow to cool for 35 to 45 minutes and top with meringue or whipped cream.

Use baking soda for grease fires in the kitchen, sprinkle on generously. i.e. dump it.

Sugar Yum Yum Pie

3 cups Sugar
1 cup Flour
1/2 tsp. Salt
2 cups Water
1/2 tsp. Cinnamon & Nutmeg

Mix all ingredients together to a creamy consistency.
Pour into a pie shell and dot with butter if desired.
Bake in a 350 degree oven until the edges of the pie are bubbly. This is a fast treat for the kids.

Meringue

Let egg white warm to room temperature. Whip until light and fluffy. Add a little at a time, 3 or 4 tablespoons of sugar. This will help meringue to stand up.

Uncle Cy's Vinegar Pie

3 Eggs (separated)
1 cup Sugar
3 tbsp. Flour
1/4 tsp. Salt
1/2 cup Vinegar
1 tsp. Lemon Flavoring (or substitute)
2 cups Boiling Water

Beat Egg Yolks until very thick. Stir in Sugar, Flour and Salt. Mix very well and add hot water, slowly. Stir constantly. Add vinegar and cook over fire until mixture thickens and is smooth. Add salt and flavoring, and pour into pie shell. Be sure that pie shell has been baked. Cover with the egg whites made into meringue. Bake in low oven (325 degrees) for 20 minutes.

Eggs should always be used at room temperature.
If an egg is called for, it usually means a large egg. Use 2 if the eggs are small.

Buying and Using Kohlrabi

This is one of the finest vegetables around. It is the best when obtained from the farmer who grows them rapidly and has plenty of water. Best picked before the weather gets too hot. When grown under these conditions, it will peel with your thumbnail. The ball will be very tender and peel much like a tangerine. The flesh is very crisp and tender. Good in the raw or cooked stage. This vegetable today is much like our cabbage. A great dish served with any meat.

Barroom Carrots

4 large Carrots (peeled)
1 tbsp. Butter
1 cup Beer (the reason for the name)
1 tsp. Sugar
1 tsp. Dill Weed (dried)

Cut the Carrots in small sticks and sauté in Butter. When barely browned, add the Beer and Dill, simmer until Carrots are tender. Stir often, add the Salt and Sugar. Cook for about 3 minutes more.   Page: 93

Kohlrabi with Cream Sauce

1 1/2 lb. Kohlrabi (6 Medium sized)
2 cups Boiling Water
3/4 tsp. Salt
2 tbsp. Butter
1 tbsp. Flour
1/4 tsp. Mustard
1 cup Milk
1/2 tsp. Salt
1/4 lb. Cheddar Cheese

Wash and clean the Kohlrabi. Cut into 1/4 inch slices in a sauce pan. Add Boiling Water and Salt. Cook uncovered for 6 to 10 minutes. Melt Butter in double boiler, blend in Flour and Mustard. Add Milk and cook over water until the mixture thickens. Add Salt and Cheese if available, add the Kohlrabi and stir only enough to coat with sauce. Serve warm.

Soak lemons and oranges in warm water before squeezing, and they will give almost twice as much juice.

Carrots – The Miracle Vegetable

Carrots have been found to be the wonder vegetable.

According to researchers, they have proven to be everything the old wives tales spoke of. Carrots can actually improve your eye sight, extend your life span, correct and prevent stress related ulcers and help prevent the risk of cancer. A study in England's Oxford University shows that carrots are the miracle veggie. The carotene and Vitamin A seem to be the reason for the importance of eating them. The recommended amount is 1 or 2 a day. Carotene and Vitamin A promote healing in general. Be cautious about eating too many carrots, because the carotene can turn your skin an orange hue.

Glazed Carrots

Follow the recipe for Cooked Carrots only add 1/2 cup of Honey.

VARIATIONS;
- You may also use 1/4 cup brown sugar.
- You may also cream the carrots by pouring a white sauce over them.

Cooked Carrots

4 medium Carrots
1 tbsp. Butter
1 cup Water
1/2 tsp. Salt
1/4 tsp. Pepper

Wash and lightly peal the Carrots. Slice into a sauce pan, cover with water. Add the seasoning and cook until tender. Try not to overcook, they are better if a little firm.

VARIATION;
- After the carrots are tender, but firm you can dip in beaten egg and roll in bread or cracker crumbs to fry.

Hot Water Pie Crust

Combine Shortening and hot water of equal amounts, and mix until foamy. Add 3 times as much Flour and 1/2 tsp. Salt. It can be rolled out while still warm, and stored in a cool place for a long time. Stir only long enough to moisten. This will be a very flaky and tender crust.

Shoo Fly Pie

This recipe is best served cold. It is a double crust pie. Take 1/3 cup Molasses and 1/3 cup boiling water. Mix with a scant, 1/2 tsp. Soda. Mix well and pour into crust. Take 1/2 cup Flour, 3/4 cups Sugar and 1/4 cup Butter. Mix together well and sprinkle over the pie. Bake 30 minutes in a 350 degree oven. Best served cold.

Karen's Carrot Pie

2 cups Cooked Carrots (mashed)
1 tsp. Cinnamon & Nutmeg
1/2 tsp. Ginger & Cloves
1 cup Thick Cream
1 tsp. Vanilla
1 tbsp. Molasses (optional)
2 Eggs (beaten)
1/4 tsp. Salt
8 tbsp. Brown Sugar

"It's a good one"

Mix Carrots and Cream together. Add flavoring and well beaten Eggs. Pour all the mixture in a pie shell and bake as you would squash or pumpkin pie. Bake at 370 degrees for 40 to 45 minutes. Test center for doneness. Bake longer if necessary. Squash, pumpkin or sweet potato can be substituted. Sprinkle top with Sugar and Cinnamon after done.

Crisp up soggy crackers by placing them on a cookie sheet and placing in a 350 degree oven for a few minutes.

This works for potato fries also.

Green Tomato Pie

6 to 8 medium Tomatoes (green)
2 tbsp. Lemon Juice
1 tsp. Lemon or Orange Rind
1/2 tsp. Salt
1/4 tsp. Cinnamon & Nutmeg
1 cup Sugar
2 tbsp. Cornstarch
1 tbsp. Lard (Shortening, or Butter)
Pastry for double pie shell

Slice the Tomatoes and remove ends and any blemishes. Combine Tomatoes with Lemon Rind Juice, Cinnamon and Nutmeg. Cook 15 minutes, stirring frequently. Combine Cornstarch and Sugar. Add to mixture, cook until clear. Be sure to stir real often. Add Lard, allow to cool slightly. Pour into pie shell and cover with top. Seal edges and bake in hot oven (425 degrees). 30 minutes should do it. Place on cookie sheet, because the pie may ooze out.

Whatever Fruit Pie
Apples, Cherries, Peaches, Boysenberries, Blueberry, Currant, Raisin, Rhubarb, etc.

4 cups Fresh Fruit (any kind)
1 or 2 cups Sugar (depends on fruit)
2 tbsp. Flour
1/4 tsp. Salt
2 tbsp. Butter
Pastry for double pie shell

If fruit is bland, add 2 tbsp. Lemon Juice. If fruit is dry, add 2 tablespoons water. Stir all ingredients into prepared fruit and toss until coated. Pour the mixture into pie shell and dot top with butter. Place 2nd crust on top and put vent holes in it with a knife or fork. Brush top with egg mixture or milk. This will give it a glazed top. Bake 20 to 30 minutes at 350 degrees.

Never pack flour in a cup to measure.
Level at top of cup for correct measurement.

Aunt Lou's Mincemeat Cookies

1/2 cup Butter (or substitute)
1/2 tsp. Baking Soda
1/2 cup Sugar
1 tsp. Cinnamon
3/4 cups Dark Molasses
1/2 tsp. Ginger
3 cups Flour (sifted)
1/2 tsp. Allspice
1/2 tsp. Salt
1 1/2 cups Mincemeat (recipe in meat section)
2 tsp. Baking Powder
1 cup Nuts (any kind)

Mix well, butter and sugar. Blend in molasses and stir in dry ingredients. Mix in mincemeat. Drop by teaspoon on greased baking sheet. Bake at 350 degrees for 12 to 15 minutes. This is a very moist cookie. Store covered. Frost if you desire.

Cowboy Cookies

1 cup Lard (or substitute)
1 cup Sugar
1 cup Brown Sugar
2 Eggs
3 cups Flour
2 cups Oatmeal
1/2 cup Milk
1 tsp. Soda
1 tsp. Baking Powder
1 tsp. Salt
Shredded Chocolate, Currants, Raisins, Dry Fruit, etc. (optional)

Cream shortening and sugars. Add eggs and mix well. Put in dry ingredients and anything else you want. Bake in a moderate oven (350 degrees) until brown (10 to 12 minutes).

This is your chance to be creative. Add whatever sounds good that you have on hand.

Cookies and milk are the way to a moms heart.

Especially at bed time. Sort of like wine and roses to a lady.

Carrot Cookies Old Fashioned

2 cups Flour
1 1/2 tsp. Baking Powder
1/4 tsp. Salt
1 tsp. Vanilla
1/2 cup Lard (or substitute)
1 Egg
1 cup Carrots (cooked and mashed)

Combine Flour, Baking Powder and Salt. Set aside. Mix Shortening and Sugar until fluffy. Add Egg, Vanilla and Carrots. Stir in Flour. Drop by teaspoon on cookie sheets. Bake in 350 degree oven for 15 to 20 minutes. These cookies can be frosted with powdered sugar frosting if desired. Very moist.

Leftover Breadcrumb Cookies

1/2 cup Lard (or substitute)
1 cup Sugar
1 Egg
2 1/2 cups Breadcrumbs
1/2 cup Flour
1 cup Cold Water
1 tsp. Nutmeg (if available)
1 tbsp. Cinnamon
1 tsp. Soda
1 cup Nuts
Raisins, Currents, Berries (any kind)
(Chocolate Chips, Coconut, etc.)

Mix in order of recipe and drop by teaspoon on cookie sheet. Flour baking sheet. Bake at 350 degree moderate temperature until brown.

Louisa's Oatmeal Drop Cookies

2 cups Flour
1 tsp. Soda
1 tsp. Salt
1 1/2 tsp. Cinnamon
2 cups Oatmeal
1 cup Lard (or substitute)
3/4 cups Brown Sugar
2 Eggs
1 tsp. Vanilla
1/3 cup Buttermilk
1 cup Dried Fruit (Currents, Raisins, Dates, Coconut, Chocolate Chips, or Butterscotch, etc.)

Mix dry ingredients and Oatmeal together. Mix Lard, Eggs, Sugars and Vanilla. Add dry ingredients and milk mixture. Combine well, and mix in misc. nut and whatever. Drop by teaspoon on greased baking sheet. Bake at moderate temperature until brown (375 degrees).

Louisa's Oatmeal Cake

1 1/2 cups Boiling Water
1 cup Oatmeal
1/2 cup Butter
1/2 cup Sugar
1/2 cup Brown Sugar
1 tsp. Nutmeg & Cinnamon
2 Eggs
1 tsp. Soda
1 tsp. Salt
1 tsp. Baking Powder
1/2 tsp. Vanilla

Put boiling water over Oatmeal and let stand for 25 minutes. Meanwhile mix together Butter, Sugar, Eggs and Vanilla, until fluffy. Sift Flour with Soda, Baking Powder, Cinnamon, Nutmeg and Salt. Add to creamed, softened oatmeal and stir. Blend well and pour into greased and floured pan. Remember not to grease the sides, it's hard to climb a greased pole. Bake for 35 minutes or until a match stick that is inserted comes out clean. Very moist.

Squash Cookies

1 cup Sugar	1/2 tsp. Cloves
1/2 cup Butter, or	1/2 tsp. Cinnamon
Shortening	1 cup Raisins or Currants
1 Egg	1 cup Nuts
2 cups Flour	1 cup Squash
1 tsp. Soda	

Mix all ingredients together and drop on cookie sheets. Bake at moderate heat (375 degrees) for 12 min.

Herder Bran Cookies

1 1/2 cups Sugar	1/2 cup Water
1 cup Molasses	1 tsp. Cinnamon
1 cup Shortening (1/2 cup	1 tsp. Soda (in a little warm
Butter or Lard)	water)
1 Egg	A pinch of Salt

Use 1/2 bran flour and 1/2 white flour. Mix enough to make a thick stiff dough. Roll very thin. Cut with cookie cutter. Add raisins or currants if desired. Bake until brown.

Gingersnaps

1 cup Sugar	1/2 lb. Sugar
	2 1/2 lb. Flour
	1/2 lb. Butter
1 tsp. Molasses	
1 tbsp. Ginger	
1 tsp. Soda	

Mix well and roll very thin. Cut into shapes and bake. Moderate oven (375 degrees).

Granny's Cinnamon Crisps

1/3 cup Shortening	1/2 tsp. Salt
1/3 cup Canned Milk	1 1/2 cups Flour
3/4 cups Sugar	1 tsp. Cinnamon
2 tsp. Baking Powder	

Cream Shortening and Sugar. Add dry ingredients, mix well and then add Milk. Roll thin, cut in fancy shapes and decorate with nuts. Bake in moderate oven (350 degrees) until light brown. These are crisp cookie.

Fresh Mountain Blueberry Cobbler

1/2 cup Sugar
1 tbsp. Cornstarch
4 cups Blueberries, Elderberries
1 tsp. Lemon Juice

In a medium sauce pan, blend Sugar and Cornstarch. Stir in Blueberries and Lemon Juice. Cook, stirring constantly until mixture comes to a boil and goes thick. Remove from fire and let cool while you prepare crust.

VARIATION;
• Sprinkle cinnamon and sugar on top of the cobbler mix.

Cobbler Crust

4 tbsp. Sugar
1 1/2 tsp. Baking Powder
1/2 tsp. Salt
1 cup Flour (sifted)
3 tbsp. Butter
2/3 cups Milk or Cream

Measure Flour, Salt, Baking Powder and Sugar into a bowl. Add Butter and Milk. Cut into mixture, the butter and mix until dough forms a ball. Spoon on to the hot fruit. Bake until the topping is golden brown. About 25 to 30 minutes. Serve with whipped cream, or ice cream or just plain. It's great any way you eat it. Oven should be around 400 degrees.

A Dutch Oven is the best way to cook a cobbler.

The heat is even and you can add brown sugar on the bottom for a double crust.

Any kind of fruit will work for cobbler.

Left Over Corn Pudding #2

2 cups Corn
2 Eggs well beaten
2 cups Milk
1/2 tsp. Sugar
1/4 tsp. Salt

Beat Eggs well & then add Corn, Milk and Seasonings. Turn into a buttered baking dish & bake at 375 degrees until dish resembles custard. Approximately 25 minutes. Check once in 20 minutes to avoid over cooking.

You can use Cream Corn too.

Ripen green tomatoes in a wet towel placed in a brown paper sack.

Blueberry Pudding Cake

1/2 cup Butter
1 cup Sugar
1 Egg
2 cups Flour
1 tsp. Baking Powder
1 tsp. Soda
1 tsp. Cinnamon
1/4 tsp. Salt
1/2 tsp. Nutmeg
1/4 tsp. Cloves
1 1/4 cups Applesauce
1 1/2 cups Blueberries

Mix Butter, Sugar and Egg to a creamy consistency. Mix all dry ingredients in a bowl and alternate mixing with Applesauce to sugar mixture. Be sure that the mixture is completely blended. Carefully fold in the Berries. Grease and flour a cooking dish or pan, remember the mix will rise a little. Cook at 350 degrees for 1 hour. Test for doneness with a broom straw or toothpick. Should pull slightly away from sides of pan. One of the best pudding cakes you will ever taste.

Apple Fritters

1 cup Sweet Milk
2 cups Flour
1 tsp. Baking Powder
2 Eggs
1/4 tsp. Salt
2 cups Chopped Apples

Put milk in a pan and heat to lukewarm. Add slowly, the eggs that have already been beaten and the flour. Stir in baking powder and salt. This should be a thick batter. Throw in apples and mix enough to cover. Drop by tsp. into hot grease. Fry to a golden brown and sprinkle with cinnamon and sugar, powdered sugar glaze or serve with maple syrup.

Apple Dumplings

1 recipe for Baking Powder Biscuits
1/2 cup Sugar
2 tsp. Nutmeg

Add the sugar to the dough while you are mixing. Roll out on floured board and sprinkle with nutmeg. Dough should be about 1/2 inch thick. Peel and core 6 med. apples. Cut dough in squares that are large enough to cover the fruit. Tuck dough in the top of the apple cavity, and put 1 tsp. sugar in each apple. Brush top with butter. In a shallow baking pan, place the apples upside down and add 1/2 cup water. Sprinkle the apples with cinnamon and sugar. Allow to bake for 10 minutes at 400 degrees. Decrease the heat and bake for 1 hour at 300 degrees. Serve warm with the sauce in the bottom of the pan. Ice cream is a great addition.

Apples were once known as God's toothbrush, but that is an old wives tale.

They have the highest content of sugar in any fruit.

Old Home Pudding Mix

2 cups Fresh Milk
1 1/2 cups Sugar
1 1/2 cups Cornstarch
1 tsp. Salt

Hold Till Later:
1 tbsp. Butter
1 tsp. Vanilla

Combine the first 4 ingredients in a sauce pan and cook over medium heat. Stir often to prevent scorching. When the 1st bubble plops, the pudding is done. Stir thoroughly and remove from heat. Stir in Butter and Vanilla. Mix enough to blend in. Pour in dishes or over a cooled cake. Serve with whipped cream or homemade Ice Cream.

Country Bread Puddin

2 cups broken up Dry Bread (sweet rolls & toast can be used)
4 cups Milk (cream is even better)
4 Eggs
1/2 cup Sugar
1 tsp. Vanilla
1/2 cup Raisins (optional)
1/2 tsp. Salt
1/4 tsp. Cinnamon & Nutmeg

Beat well, Milk, Eggs, Vanilla, Sugar & Salt. Pour mixture over crumpled up bread mixture, pour in greased 2 qt. pan. Sprinkle Nutmeg and Cinnamon on top. Bake 1 hour or until knife comes out clean. Serve with whipped cream, lemon sauce or milk.

If a dish should scorch, add 1/2 tsp. of sugar to help remove the scorch taste.

Prairie Pudding
(Carrot or Plum)

Sift together:
1 cup Sugar
1 cup Flour
1 tsp. Cinnamon, Nutmeg & Soda
3/4 tsp. Salt
2 tsp. Cream of Tartar

Now add:
1 cup raw Carrots and Potatoes
1/2 cup Cooking Oil
1 cup Nuts
2 cups Raisins

Mix thoroughly all ingredients. Grease up cans of the #1 size and fill 2/3 full. Loaf pans can be substituted Steam in a 350 degree oven for 2 hours. Check for doneness by inserting a toothpick or broom straw. If it comes out clean it's done. To steam means placing a pan or cans of water in the oven with pudding. This will keep the moisture in the pudding. Serve with whipped cream or lemon sauce.

Rhubarb Pudding

Make up old home pudding recipe (on page 99) and a put thin layer in a bowl. Now in a pan on the stove cook together, 2 cups Rhubarb and 1 cup Brown Sugar. Add just enough water to make paste. Simmer until Rhubarb is transparent or done. Cool and put a thin layer on pudding. Sprinkle with a little Cinnamon and Nutmeg. Cover with more pudding and another layer of Rhubarb. Sprinkle with more Cinnamon, Nutmeg and Sugar. Serve with whipped cream or on a slice of rhubarb cake.

1/2 cup shortening plus 1/4 tsp. salt can be substituted for 1/2 cup butter.

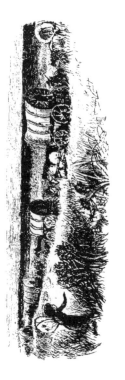

Old Squaw Indian Pudding
This is a Navajo recipe

3 pts. Sweet Milk
2 large iron spoons of Yellow Cornmeal
2 small Eggs
1 iron spoon of Molasses
3/4 cups Sugar
1 tsp. plus a pinch of Ginger
1 level tsp. full Cinnamon
1/2 tsp. Nutmeg
1/2 cup thick Sour Cream

In an open kettle over the fire, put half of the Milk. Be sure to add a sprinkle of salt to the milk. As soon as the milk comes to a boil, quickly scatter the Corn Meal over the milk. Do this evenly by hand. Remove immediately from the fire to a dish and pour in the cold Milk. Now add the Egg well beaten, the Spices, Molasses, Sugar and Sour Cream. Pour into bake dish and put in oven. Bake hot the first 1/2 hour and moderate the last part of baking time. 425 degrees then 300 degrees, bake 3 hours.

If this pudding is done right, it will be delicious.

In a Dutch oven when you smell it - it's done

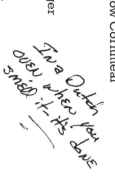

The Indians were thrifty people that lived off the land, never wasted, and took care of what they needed.

REMEMBER 4 THINGS FOR SUCCESS;
- The eggs must be fairly small
- The pudding should be runny when poured into the baking dish
- The baking time is very important
- You should be hungry and ready for a special treat

Baked Rhubarb

3 cups Rhubarb
1 cup Sugar
2 tbsp. Butter

Wash and cut Rhubarb into 1 inch pieces. Put Sugar and Butter on top of Rhubarb in a baking dish. Bake for 45 minutes at 325 degrees.

Turnips

When you eat a turnip, you are actually eating the root. These are extremely versatile and tasty vegetable. Wash and clean the plant as you would carrots. Peel and cut into pieces. Cover in a pan with enough water to boil. Add salt, pepper and a little butter. Cook until tender. Can be mashed and eaten as you would mashed potatoes.

Stuffed Onions

2 large Onions
1 recipe for Meatloaf (P27)
1/2 tsp. Salt
Pepper to taste
1/2 cup Celery (chopped)
6 or 8 slices of Green Pepper

Peel skin from sides of Onion. Carefully cut down the side of the onion to the center. Peel the layers of the onion off so as not to break if possible. Form the onion slices around the balls of meatloaf. In a pan, that has been greased, place the Green Pepper slices and put the stuffed onion on top of each. Sprinkle a small amount of Salt and Pepper on top and a few pinches of Celery. Put a little water in the pan, about 1/3 cup and spread the rest of the celery in the bottom for taste. Bake at 325 for 25 to 35 minutes depending on the size of the onion.

While cooking foods that have an unpleasant odor, boil a pan of water with vinegar in it. It will absorb odors.

Watercress Soup

6 tbsp. Butter
3 Potatoes
1 cup Celery (chopped)
1 medium Onion
4 cups Water
2 1/2 cups Watercress
1/2 tsp. Salt
3 tbsp. Chicken Base
1/2 cup Sour Cream

Melt 2 tbsp. of Butter in a pan on the stove. Add the Celery and Onion already chopped to the butter. Simmer for 2 to 3 minutes. Peel and cut up Potatoes, add to the onion mixture. Now add the Watercress, the Water, Salt, Pepper and Chicken Base. Simmer for 30 minutes. Allow to cool slightly. Beat well with wire whip or run thru a grinder to puree. Let cool completely. When ready to serve, heat and add the other 4 tbsp. of butter and sour cream. Use wire whip again and mix well. Remove from heat and check seasoning, add more if necessary. Serve warm.

Substitute grated Cucumbers for Water Cress

Quick Country Carrots

1 1/4 lbs. New Carrots
3 tbsp. Butter
1/4 cup Honey
1/2 tsp. Salt, Pepper
1/3 cup Water

Clean Carrots and slice or cut in whatever shape or size you desire. Combine Carrots, Water and Butter in pan. Cover and cook till tender. Add Honey, Salt and Pepper. Allow to simmer just a few minutes longer for the taste to be all thru the carrots. Do not cook till mushy.

Wilted celery, lettuce and dandelion greens can be revived by soaking in cold water and adding a few drops of lemon juice. Soak only a short time.

Cactus Jelly

3 cups Cactus Juice and Pulp
1/2 cup Lemon Juice
1 pkg. Pectin
4 1/2 cups Sugar

Wash and scald fruits, remove the spots but not the prickles. Cut in half and cover with barely enough water to go over the fruit. Cook 15 minutes and strain thru bag to squeeze out juice. Mix in pectin. Bring to a boil. Cook for 1 1/2 minutes, stirring. Remove from heat, put in jars and seal with wax.

Prickly Pear Cactus

How Sweet It Is

The prickly pear is a member of the cacti family. The stems of the plant are flat. The flower appears from April to June. The fruit develops below the flower. To eat the stem, slice it off very carefully. The spines are sharp and hooked. The hooked spines will work their way into your skin so be sure to use gloves and caution. Split the stem length wise and scoop out the pulp to eat. Also great as Cactus Jelly (See the recipe on this page).

You can buy prickly pear cactus in "I" larges
Super Markets, Too!

Cactus Candy
(This is a Delightfully Different Treat)

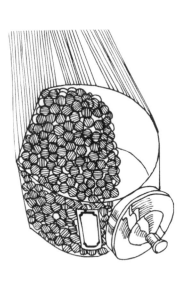

Use only Barrel cactus when making candy. Try to find a nice fat, healthy cactus. This is important, because only the pulp inside is used. Cut the cactus into 1 inch slices and take out the core. Cut pulp into small pieces and boil for about 4 or 5 hours. Drain thoroughly and dry. Mix 1/2 Sugar and 1/2 Corn syrup together in enough liquid to cover the pulp. Cook the pulp and syrup mixture for about an hour, and allow to stand for another day. Then cook until the syrup threads. It should look like preserves when ready to crystallize.

When this has been done, mix another pan with 2 parts sugar and 1 part syrup. Stir until it is cloudy. While it is still milky looking, stir well and take cactus pulp which has been broke into squares after spread out and allowed to cool in thin layers on a buttered pan or wax paper. Drop each piece into the syrup mixture for a minute or two and remove with wire thongs and place on screen or wax paper to dry. Remember not to place to close as it will stick together in a mass. The average Barrel Cactus that you should use will weigh about 25 to 30 pounds. These cacti should not be wasted, so be prepared to make a large batch. These cacti contain water that could save a life so do not waste them. They cannot be taken from a protected area. Know where you are before you cut it down. Obey your laws.

Marshmallows

2 Envelopes Clear Gelatin
1/2 cup Cold Water
1/2 tsp. Salt
2 cups Sugar
1 tsp. Vanilla
3/4 cups Boiling Water

Boil Sugar and Water until syrup tests thread stage. Remove from fire, soften Gelatin in cold water. Add hot syrup and stir until dissolved. Let stand until partially cooled. Add Salt and Flavoring. Beat until mixture becomes thick fluffy & cold. Thickly cover the bottom of an 8 x 4 pan with powdered sugar. Pour in mixture. Let it stand in a cool place (not refrigerated) until thoroughly cool. With wet sharp knife, loosen around edges of the pan and turn out on board lightly covered with powdered sugar. Cut into cubes and roll in powered sugar.

Mallow Corn and Nuts

When marshmallow mixture is ready to pour in pan and be cut in squares, pour over already popped corn and any kind of nuts that are available. This is a special treat for company or kids.

Water Cress -- Roomy Salad

1/3 cup Oil
2 tbsp. TarragonWhite WineVinegar
Pepper to taste
7 cups Watercress
2 cups Mushrooms

Mix oil and Vinegar in bowl, add Wine and seasonings. Slice in Mushrooms and Cress. Serve immediately. This is a great fresh salad.

Baking soda will sweeten cream that has soured.

Add a pinch at a time until cream reaches desired sweetness.

Corn Meal Mush - Fried

3 cups Yellow Corn Meal
2 qts, Boiling Water
Salt to taste

Slowly add corn meal to already boiling water. Stirring constantly until the corn meal is blended well. Stir mixture a few minutes longer to make sure it is blended, and then cover and simmer for 2 to 4 hours. Poor into oblong pan, and slice when cool. Fry slowly in a pan with lard and butter. When brown lightly, serve with hot maple syrup.

Hoarhound Candy

3 1/2 lbs. Brown Sugar
3 cups Hot Water
3 ounces Hoarhound
A dash of Salt

Bring water to a boil, and add hoarhound flavoring. Slowly boil for 20 minutes. Cook until syrup forms a hard ball when tested in a cup of cold water. Pour the mixture into a shallow pan that has been greased. When cool, form into small pieces and cut into squares. This can be rolled in sugar when cut.

Old Old-Recipe's !
Just like me! - I
remember right - I'm thinking

Whenever possible, use a wooden spoon to stir your candies.

Hot syrup candies have a tendency to heat metal spoons and make them hard to hold.

Long handled wooden spoons will prevent burns.

LOG CABIN BLUES

Soups
Vegetables
Miscellaneous

Helpful Hints or Remedies for All Cures:

1. (1584) The hickot is cured by suddennewes of strange things

2. (1626) Sneezing doth cure the hiccough

3. (1727) You must at the time of a hickup seize and pull the ring finger

4. Cover your head with a pillow, to cure hiccups

5. Spit on a rock and turn it over, to cure hiccups

6. Eat a spoonful of peanut butter, to cure hiccups

7. Eat a spoonful of sugar, salt, vinegar or Worcestershire Sauce

8. Eat finely crushed ice

9. Drink water thru a folded hanky

10. Drink a glass of water upside down

11. Breathe into a paper bag

12. Stand on your head and drink a glass of water

An apple cut in half and placed in storage with a cake will help keep it fresh longer.

Hot Buttered Rum

1 lb. Butter (melted)
1 tsp. Allspice
1 tsp. Nutmeg
1 tsp. Ground Cloves
1 tsp. Cinnamon
2 lb. Dark Brown Sugar
3 Eggs (beaten)

Melt Butter and add spices. Pour over Brown Sugar and let cool. Mix beaten Eggs with sugar mixture (low speed for 1/2 hour). Place in jar, seal, and refrigerate. Place 1 tbsp. batter in cup of hot water and stir with cinnamon stick.

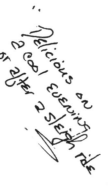

Delicious on a cool evening or after a sleigh ride

To remove tarnish from brass and copper, rub with a fresh cut lemon.

Sweetened Condensed Milk

1/4 cup Butter or Substitute
1 cup very hot Water
4 cups Powdered Milk
2 cups Sugar

Melt Butter in water. Mix all ingredients thoroughly. Beat till smooth and thick. Will be just like today's Eagle Brand Milk. Will store for a long time in your refrigerator. Great for cooking.

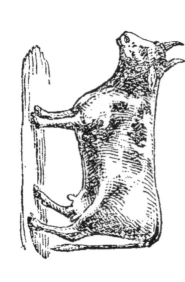

Nut Brittle

1 1/2 cups Sugar
1/4 cup Corn Syrup
A pinch of Salt
1/2 cup Water
2 pinches of Soda
2 tbsp. Butter
3/4 cups Nuts
1 1/2 tsp. Vanilla

Combine 1st 4 ingredients, stirring constantly until sugar is dissolved. Bring to a boil, cook until a small amount dropped in a glass of water turns real brittle. Remove from heat and add the Soda, Butter and Nuts of your choice. Or, add 2 or 3 different kinds of nuts. Stir enough to mix and then pour onto a thin buttered sheet pan. As the candy cools, break into small pieces. Be sure to pour candy as thin as possible.

White Taffy

2 cups Sugar
1/2 cup Corn Syrup
2/3 cups Water
1 tsp. Vanilla

Put all ingredients in a pan, and cook until it reaches the hard stage. This will break when added to the cool water. Stir only until sugar dissolves. Cool and add Vanilla. Pour onto a cookie sheet that has been greased. When cool, pick up taffy with greased hands and pull. Be careful not to pull it if it is too hot, as it will burn your hands. It's a lot of fun to have a taffy pull at parties.

Did you know? Cooking in cast iron definitely boosts your iron intake.

Soup simmered for a few hours in an iron pot,

has almost 20 times as much iron as soup cooked in another pot.

Cracker Jacks

2 cups Sugar
3 cups Popped Corn
1 cup Molasses
1 1/2 cups Nuts
2 tbsp. Vinegar
1/2 tsp. Soda

- Such a treat

Boil 1st 3 ingredients in a pan, until it cracks when tested in cold water. Remove from fire and add Soda. Pour over already Popped Corn and Nuts of your choice.

Easy to Make Popcorn Balls

1 lb. Marshmallow
1/3 cup Butter
12 cups Popped Corn (salted)
Coloring (if desired)

Melt butter in pan, add Marshmallows and melt down. Bring to a boil and stir well to prevent scorching. Pour over Popped Corn that has been salted. Color syrup if you wish. Fold to cover all the corn and wet hands in cold water before shaping into balls. Hot syrup can burn, handle carefully.

When butter is called for in a recipe, it can be substituted with margarine.

White Sauce

2 cups Milk
1/2 tsp. Finely Minced Onion
1/4 cup Butter
3 tbsp. Flour
Salt and Pepper to taste

Bring the Milk to simmer, add the Onion, Salt and Pepper. Melt butter in pan, stir in Flour. Add the flour mixture to milk mixture. Continue to simmer until mixture thickens, about 10 minutes. Low, low heat so's not to scorch milk.

White sauce is excellent over almost any vegetable.

Instant White Sauce

Blend together 1 cup Flour & 1 cup soft Butter. Spread into ice cube tray & chill well. Cut into cubes and store in the freezer. This should make about 16 cubes. When in need of white sauce, drop into 1 cup of milk, and heat slowly. Add seasonings and let simmer. Stir and let thicken.

VARIATIONS:
- Add boiled eggs chopped up and put over toast.
- Add tuna fish and put over toast.
- Chopped beef over toast.
- Use as gravy over meats, and let your imagination work for you.

*Great Gravy
for Biscuits cooked
Salmon + 1cup 1tsp sage*

White sauce is thought to have been invented by the Greeks.

Graham Crackers

4 cups Graham Flour
3/4 cups Brown Sugar
1/2 cup Shortening
2 tsp. Baking Powder
1/2 tsp. Salt

Mix all ingredients together well. Brush dough with Milk, and roll into thin cakes. Use white flour to roll the dough with. Cut into squares, & bake in hot oven till crisp.

When a recipe calls for pumpkin pie spice, it means a mixture of nutmeg, cinnamon, cloves and ginger.

Log Cabin Noodles

2 Eggs (well beaten)
1/2 tsp. Salt
2 tbsp. Water
1/2 tsp. Baking Powder

Mix all ingredients together and add just enough Flour to make a stiff dough. Roll out to a thin crust, let stand for several hours until dough begins to dry a bit. You can now fold it over in layers and slice it to the width you desire. Some can be thin and some fat. Spread apart and allow to thoroughly dry.

Is a dripping faucet keeping you awake? Tie a string around the tap that is long enough to reach the sink. The water will run quietly along the string until you can fix it.

Homemade Mayonnaise

2 tsp. Vinegar or Lemon Juice
1 cup Oil
A small dash Red Pepper
1 Egg Yolk
1/2 tsp. Mustard
1/2 tsp. Salt

Chill a dish & beat the Egg Yolk with a wood or silver spoon. When the Egg is well beaten, add the seasonings and the oil one drop at a time. Beat well after each drop. Do not reverse the motion. When the dressings begin to thicken, add the Vinegar or the Lemon Juice one drop at a time. Continue beating until all oil and acids are well consumed. Be sure to have the dishes and ingredients as cool as possible. If the mixture should begin to curdle, begin immediately with a fresh egg, in a fresh dish, cooled, beat it well and carefully add one drop at a time to the curdled mixture. Keep dish cool. If necessary, set the dish in ice.

Cooked mayo can be used for those who do not like oil.

VARIATIONS;

White Mayonnaise

If you desire the mayo to be white, just follow the original recipe and use lemon juice instead of vinegar. Take the mustard out altogether, and when it is finished, add a half cup of whipped cream or an egg white beaten very stiff.

Green Mayonnaise

Chop parsley leaves very fine and pound them in a small amount of lemon juice. Strain and add the juice to the mayo. This will turn it light green. Looks great on the dandelion leaves or lettuce.

Red Mayonnaise

Mash one scant tbsp. of lobster coral thru a fine strainer (sieve) and add it to the dressing. Mash 1/2 Red Pepper & add this today.

Preserving Walnuts

Shell the walnuts. Place them in a pt. jar. You can separate the whole and broken ones as you shell. Soak lids in hot water for 10 minutes. Put on jars and bake for 30 minutes in a warm (250 degree) oven. Do not open the oven until time is up. If the oven door is opened, it will cause the nuts to sweat and mildew. Do not fill jar too full so the lid will set tight, and seal. Use up soon or reseal, if they do not seal at first.

Baked Peaches

Plunge the peaches into boiling water. This will loosen the skins. Peel, cut in half, and lay cut side up on a baking dish or pan. Fill the centers with butter and sugar, a few drops of lemon juice, and a sprinkle of cinnamon and nutmeg. Bake 15 to 20 minutes and serve warm on toast or with Ice Cream.

Snow Ice Cream

2 cups Milk or Cream
2 Eggs
1 1/2 cups Sugar
1/2 tsp. Salt
3 tsp. Vanilla

Whip all ingredients together and add clean snow until no more can be added. Then put in dishes and add topping if desired. A special treat for kids.

Brine for Curing Meat

4 gallons of Water
8 lb. Salsta (not table salt)
3 lb. Sugar
3 oz. Salt Peter

This will cure about 100 lbs. of meat. Mix together in a large drum. Prepare meat in size you desire, and lower into the brine. Be sure that you stir before adding meats to dissolve the ingredients, and after adding meat to coat each piece. This is especially good for pork.

Money isn't everything,

but it does encourage our children to keep in touch.

Mom's cooking always brought me home for the holidays.

Potato Chips

Wash and peel several potatoes, cut them into thin slices and dry thoroughly in a cloth. Put into a well buttered bag. Fasten the bag with clips and place in a very hot oven. The chips should be brown in about 15 minutes. Turn the bag over several times to assure even browning.

(This is part of *Paper Bag Cooking*.)

POULTRY SEASONING

When a recipe calls for poultry seasoning, it will have in it the following; Thyme, Sage, Margrum, Rosemary, Pepper & Nutmeg. Simply add a pinch of each to your dish or omit the ones you don't like.

Dandelion Coffee

Loosen dirt around the plant and pull up roots and all. Wash the plant well, and pull apart. Discard seeds and stems, put leaves in lemon water for salads, and roast the roots in an open oven for 4 to 5 hours, or until they have shriveled. When dry, they will crack crisply when broken. Inside they are brown like coffee beans. Grind the roots and use as you would ground coffee beans.

Greens

Wash young tender leaves. Cut in to small pieces. Cut up several strips of bacon fried crisp. Pour over the top of the greens. Add salt and pepper to taste. Very good with chili or stews.

DANDELION

Root

Stem

Seed

Leaf

One pinch of salt in the pot with your coffee, will take out any unpleasant bitterness.

Buttermilk Tips for Cooking

- Sour milk can stand in for buttermilk in any recipe. To sour milk, add one tbsp. of fresh lemon juice or vinegar to one cup of room temperature milk. Be sure to let stand for 20 minutes or more. The milk will start to form curds. This process will not work with bottled juice.

- Buttermilk has a long shelf life, but it will separate as it sits. Be sure to shake well before using it. It adds a real special taste to your cooking.

- Cultured powered buttermilk is a great product to keep on hand. It can be found in most stores. Mixing pancakes is a cinch with this product. All dry ingredients can be mixed up ahead of time and stored in a plastic bag. Then just add water for great instant pancakes while camping.

- If you want to substitute sweet milk for buttermilk in a recipe, just remember that all buttermilk baked goods need a small amount of baking soda to neutralize buttermilk acidity. Use 1/2 tsp. soda for each cup of buttermilk.

Don't forget how good Vinegar can be for you and how many purposes it can be used for.

Remember to

Cook with Love

in each and every recipe.

This way you'll always have Love in your home

Burned food stuck on any aluminum pan, can be removed by boiling an onion & 3 tbsp Vinegar in water.

Why Does Soap Make You Clean?

Sometimes it seems like a bother to use soap. But, it does make us cleaner than plain water. There are small valleys and hollow spots in our skin. Dirt gets in these and plain water cannot get it out. It may wash out some of these, but not all. But soap works in a different way. It pulls dirt out. When you mix soap with water, great things happen. The soap and water foam to make those wonderful bubbles. Each bubble is like a little balloon, and when you make it lather, you are simply pumping air into the soapy water. A soap bubble does not seem very strong, but it can pick up dirt. Soap bubbles act somewhat like magnets as they pick up dirt. They pull it away from your skin. Soap lather has many bubbles in it. Each one can pick up a bit of dirt, and then the rinse water can carry the dirt away.

Factories make soap from chemicals and oil. In the old days, people made soap from wood ashes, water, and grease that was left over from meat that they cooked. Imagine that, ashes get you dirty, and grease gets you dirty. But when you put them in the same pot with water and cook them down... you have a soap which washes dirt away.

When your hands are badly stained from working in your garden or on a car, put a tbsp. of sugar or salt on your hands with the soap. The lather will surprise you.

Old Western Green Tomato Catsup

8 qts. Green Tomatoes
4 qts. White Onions
2 oz. Mustard Seed
1/2 tsp. Allspice
4 cups Brown Sugar
1 oz. Cloves
1/2 cup Dry Mustard
1/4 cup Water
1 oz. Pepper
1 oz. Celery
Vinegar

Chop Tomatoes and Onions, sprinkle with salt. Let stand 3 hours. Drain well to remove all juice. Put all other ingredients in pot. Cover with Vinegar and simmer for 1 hour. Ready to eat. Can be sealed in jars if desired. Will keep in cool place for days.

Dandelion Green Salad

1 cup Dandelion Greens
1 head of lettuce
2 Tomatoes
1 Cucumber
1 Spanish Red Onion
2/3 cups Salad Dressing

Wash and crisp all greens. Break into pieces. Cut Tomatoes into pieces and add to salad. Slice Onion and Cucumber in small thin pieces and put in salad. Toss with salad dressing. Mayonnaise and sour cream dressing with seasoning is very good on this salad.

Fried Tomatoes

Slice Tomatoes rather thick. Sprinkle with Salt and Pepper, Flour and fry in butter. Lay on warm platter and pour a cream sauce (page 103) over them. Excellent with most meat dishes.

If vegetables are wilted, sprinkle with cold water and wrap in a towel.

Refrigerate for an hour and they will freshen right up.

Tomato Soup

6 Ripe Tomatoes (chopped)
2 tbsp. Butter or Oil
3 cups Chicken Soup Stock
1 cup Milk or Cream
Salt and Pepper to taste
Butter
Celery Leaves

Sauté tomatoes in butter until tender. Mix with soup stock, simmer for 20 minutes. Beat mixture with egg beater and return to fire. Add milk or cream and a little more butter. Heat and serve with celery leaves on top.

The Mushroom

Mushrooms can be very dangerous, so do not try to go out and gather them if you are not sure of what you have. This is considered one of mans most glorious foods.

The Tomato

I cannot imagine what the Americans would do without tomatoes. Used in Pizza, Catsup, Tomato Sauce, Soups, and Spaghetti. There are too many things to mention. This American fruit was brought here by the colonists and enjoyed by the likes of Tom Jefferson. He actually grew these at Monticello, and named 4 or 5 varieties. The tomato was at one time considered poisonous. Today it is used for almost everything.

Sautée mushrooms in butter,
and sprinkle with Parmesan Cheese.
It's a marvelous appetizer.

Rules for cooking mushrooms:

- Do not wash unless you have to
- Do not peel
- Do not soak
- Do not overcook
- The quickest way to clean a mushroom is to use a damp cloth

9-Mile Heritage Expeditions

Linking the Past to the Future
BY
Teaching Traditional Back Country Skills

Come join us at 9-mile for a day or a week of great fun. You may want to participate in Horsemanship and packing classes, Horse Handling and training, Cross-cut saw maintenance, Cross-cut saw certification, Use and care of traditional tools, Basic Horsemanship, Defensive Horsemanship, Leave no Trace stock course, Ninemile packing clinics, Advanced Horsemanship, Advanced Packing Classes or the Traditional Low Impact Back Country Cooking done with Dutch Ovens.

You can learn a lot, eat a lot of good cooking, meet some of the world's best people, make new friends, hear great campfire music and do it all in the beautiful Montana mountains. 9-Mile is located about 20 miles west of Missoula, and 4 miles off the main highway. You can wake up to the mules morning serenade, have elk and deer in your front yard, stimulating crisp country morning air and enjoy some of the best conversation you'll ever here.

I am privileged to be the one who teaches the Dutch Oven classes and help feed the crew most of the classes. It's my home away from home and I love it. Chad, Bob, Laura and almost anyone at 9-Mile will do their best to make you feel welcome. If you go away hungry it's my fault. If you want more info., just call the Ranger station and they will send you a brochure.

Or write to:

Heritage Expeditions
20325 Remount Rd.
Huson, MT 59846
Phone: (406) 626-5201

Thanks Colleen

Help
Montana's First Dude Ranch

We want to **save** this old *Historic* Ranch.

The OTO needs your help.
Labor & Financial help are needed.

One hundred years ago, Dick Randall, started the fist Dude Ranch in Montana. The OTO became one of the first of its kind and is credited with putting the "Dude" in Dude Ranch. Now after many years of neglect, the 30 plus buildings on the ranch need our help.

This major piece of Western History will disappear unless we work together to save it.

For more information contact us at;
Dude Ranch Montana
PO Box 259
Gardiner Montana 59030

Phone:
406-580-8767
801-571-0789
208-743-5874

E-Mail:
WGoutermont
@hotmail.com